CANT BE WRONG

Other books by the author:

What Withers, Doones Press, 1970
The Lines Are Drawn, Asphalt Press, 1970
mcmlxvi poem, The Nomad Press, 1970
Stupid Rabbits, Morgan Press, 1971
The South Orange Sonnets, Some of Us Press, 1972
Late Sleepers, Pellet Press, 1973
Malenkov Takes Over, A Dry Imager Publication, 1974
Sex/The Swing Era, Lucy & Ethel, 1975
My Life, Wyrd Press, 1975
Mentally, He's a Sick Man, Salt Lick Press, 1975
Oomaloom, A Dry Imager Publication, 1975
Dues, The Stonewall Press, 1975
Rocky Dies Yellow, Blue Wind Press, 1975, second edition 1977
None of the Above (Editor), Crossing Press, 1976
Charisma, O Press, 1976
In the Mood, Titanic Books, 1978
Just Let Me Do It, Vehicle Editions, 1978
Catch My Breath, Salt Lick Press, 1978, second edition 1995
White Life, Jordan Davies, 1980
Hollywood Magic, Little Caesar, 1982
Attitude, Hanging Loose Press, 1982

& the solo compact disc recording:
What You Find There, New Alliance Records, 1994

CANT BE WRONG

POEMS BY MICHAEL LALLY 1985-1992

COFFEE HOUSE PRESS :: MINNEAPOLIS :: 1996

Cover design by Susan Campbell of CAMPBELL design.
Cover art is a painting of Miles Lally by his sister Caitlin.
Back cover photograph by Robert Zuckerman.
Book design by Chris Fischbach.

Some of these poems have appeared in *Arshille, Shiny, The St. Mark's Poetry Project Newsletter, Salt Lick, The Hollywood Review, Forkroads,* in the anthology *Grand Passion* (Red Wing Books), and on the compact disc *What You Find There* (New Alliance Records).

Coffee House Press is supported in part, by a grant provided by the Minnesota State Arts Board, through an appropriation by the Minnesota State Legislature, and by a grant from the National Endowment for the Arts, a federal agency. Additional support has been provided by the Lila Wallace-Reader's Digest Fund; The McKnight Foundation; Lannan Foundation; Target Stores, Dayton's, and Mervyn's by the Dayton Hudson Foundation; General Mills Foundation; St. Paul Companies; Honeywell Foundation; Star Tribune/Cowles Media Company; Beverly J. And John A. Rollwagen Fund of The Minneapolis Foundation; Prudential Foundation; and The Andrew W. Mellon Foundation.

Coffee House Press books are available to the trade through our primary distributor, Consortium Book Sales & Distribution, 1045 Westgate Drive, Saint Paul, Mn 55114. For personal orders, catalogs or other information, write to:

> Coffee House Press
> 27 North Fourth Street, Suite 400
> Minneapolis, MN 55401

ISBN 1-56689-046-2

10   9   8   7   6   5   4   3   2   1

TABLE OF CONTENTS

Thanks to Karen Allen, Ed Begley Jr., Eve Bransdstein, Ray DiPalma, Jim Haining, Michael Harris, Joan Hopewell, Helena Kallianiotes, David Milch, Michael O'Keefe, Aram Saroyan, Hubert Selby Jr., Robert Slater, Rita Stern, Terence Winch, and especially Kristal Rogers.

And in memory of Joan Baribeault, Ted Berrigan, Joe Brainard, Ed Cox, Ralph Dickey, Tim Dlugos, Cliff Heard, Sissie Johnson, Etheridge Knight, James Schuyler, and all the Lallys who have passed away since I was a boy, including my parents, my sister Joan, my brother James, and the mother of my children, Lee Lally.

Dedicated to my children:
Caitlin Maeve Lally & Miles Aaron Lally

1

GETTING READY TO HAVE BEEN LOVED

(A POET'S LIFE)

GOING HOME AGAIN

Last week I flew into Albany where
it was cold and there was snow on
the ground—I was met by my
daughter and son who drove me to
Vermont where they go to college
—she was 21 that day and I was
there to give her 21 little presents
to make up for the years when I was
so busted I couldn't give her much,
or was so stoned I couldn't get it
together on time—the delight in
her face when she realized after
the first one, when I pretended I
forgot something and pulled out
another and then another and so on
until she got that there were 21—
even my son got hip to the fun of
our little scene, despite all he's
going through at 19 I thought he
might be able to avoid because he
doesn't have to live the way I
thought I did when I was his age—
but maybe I didn't have to either,
what do I know?—so I go down to
New York for some fun, I guess,
trying to avoid the social mess I
made the last time I stayed with
my kids when one of their friends
made it clear she thought I was
more than the dear old dad of a
friend and I didn't resist—in

fact I insisted we could find a
place to be alone, like my
daughter's room when she wasn't
home—but that isn't the point
of this poem, this isn't about
my most recent dating trends,
but something even harder to
comprehend, unless you can remember
a time when there were no hippies
no homeless no dozens of mixed
couples, black and white, walking
the streets like lovers, or even
just friends—and unless you were
living on those streets too,
looking for a way to get through
the night without a fight with some
thug and you, I mean me, just
looking for someone to hug and
not knowing it—this was before
Naked Lunch or *Last Exit to
Brooklyn,* long before Dylan and
John Doe and all those other artists
we admire for the truth started
lying about their names—I'm talkin'
about before Martin Luther King's
"I Have a Dream" speech, before the
Cuban crisis and The Beatles,
a time when Dixie Peach could
still be found on the heads of
most black people, who were still
called "colored" or "Negro" but
on the streets the term was "spade"
and I had one tattooed on my arm
in defiance of the Jersey whites

who kept me in constant fights
over my preference for black girls
once I had discovered the lack of
bullshit in romancing them—unlike
their white counterparts there was
no time or reason to play games,
nobody was taking anybody home to
anybody's mother, or the prom or
even the corner hangout—if we dug
each other it meant secret lovers
and that was it, hell even the
black dudes were ready to pick up
sticks and hit you upside the head
for messing with Sapphire—but
somehow I survived and made it to
the streets of Greenwich Village
where a handful of perverts and
junkies and thieves and dreamers
created a community of lost souls
with room for me in it—and for
Pauline the 15-year-old light-skinned
runaway from Long Island City with
a body that everybody noticed even
when it became clear she was pregnant
—I remember thinking how brave
she was to be out there alone like
that—you got to remember there was
only a handful of us on the streets
then—runaways got arrested, and
blacks were especially unwelcome
except by a handful of whites we
couldn't figure out, even though I
was one of them—only there were no
other white boys on the streets

falling in love with black girls
and letting the world know it then,
although every time I talk or write
about it out here in Hollywood,
these producers and directors and
executives I run into who are my age
all claim yeah, they were doing
the same thing—only I guess it was
in some really hip suburb somewhere
in the Midwest, because I lived
on the streets of Manhattan then and
take my word for it, there was no
other white teenaged boy out there
with a black teenaged girl taking
the shit you got even there from
the assholes who couldn't understand
something I'm still trying to figure
out—and they weren't on the streets
of DC or Chicago or Detroit or St.
Louis or any of the other cities I
ended up running in or running away
to—but first I fell for a doe-eyed
dark-skinned thin-wristed Indian-nosed
beautiful black girl from Atlantic City
who had just moved into an apartment
on Tompkins Square—I saw her in a
bar called Obie's on Sixth Avenue
that I only figured out years later,
long after I hung out there, was named
for the awards they give for Off-Broadway
Theater, something I thought only the
rich and the snobby, or as the spades
said, the siddidy, went to back then—
what did I know? not much except the

glow in those deep dark eyes when she
looked into mine and I knew there'd
never be a time when I couldn't see them
burning in my mind, and I was right,
there never has been—so there I was
in the city again, and it's almost
thirty years later—we still keep in
touch, running our subsequent women
and men by each other every few years—
we even dated once almost ten years ago
and it was still there, the glow, but
I was more aware that time of what had
scared me back then, a kind of crazy
independence that made her unpredictable
—we were so young, not even 20 yet, and
the world was trying to kick my ass so
bad for loving her, even my spade bros
pulled my coat constantly over what
they thought was my inappropriate
fixation on this one lover, they used to
call me "Porgy" after we broke up and
I would wander into bars all over
Manhattan looking for her—bars like
Obie's or Pat's on 23rd near Sixth where
she tells me to meet her at midnight
last Friday, she's coming down from
what used to be part of Harlem and
is now part of "The Upper West Side"
with Pauline, they're still friends
ever since I introduced them—and I
show up wearing almost the same clothes
I was wearing back then, my hair not
much different, just gray where it used
to be black, but not her, she's black

where she always was, her hair, her skin,
her eyes—Pauline I wouldn't recognize,
she's a queen-sized grandmother still bitching
about her crazy friend, with that kind of
mock toughness that covers love so deep
and lasting it can't be described—the
kind I'm feeling as I look into Bambi's
eyes and I see this 17-year-old girl
still looking back at me, and I got to
take her hand and kiss it and she says
"Hey, that's what made me fall for you
the first time we met" and I can't forget
anything, even though we argue about the
details of that first night we don't
argue anymore about the rest, especially
the best which we both remember together
as she says how glad she is that she
picked me to be the first—something
I didn't believe for years, I just didn't
trust her, because I didn't trust myself,
the act I was playing back then, can you
imagine, a skinny little white kid from
New Jersey trying to act like a man when
all I wanted to do was look into those
eyes forever, maybe even cry a little
at the wonder of it all, but instead I
took on the world that tried to make us
wrong—I thought that was the way to be
strong—even after she took on two other lovers
—even when she wrote and told me she was
pregnant from one of them—I remember I
got some leave and made it to the city,
I was a serviceman then, with no stripes,
from getting into fights and court-martialed,

and I end up at this bar where a guy we
called "Joe the Puerto Rican," another kid
from the streets I knew, and his girl known
as "Girl," says "Hey there's Bambi's old
man" and I slam the bar and say "Don't
call me that" and he says "Oh man if you
hate that bitch now, you'll be glad to hear
this, she's in this crib on 14th Street
and she's all alone and fucked up man,
she ain't so hot shit no more like she usta
been——" and I guess I wasn't just a
poser back then like some of my newfound
friends, 'cause he couldn't even see the
rage that was building in me toward him
that I was sitting on as he kept talking
"——hey man, you probably dig to see her,
fuck her ass up man, I can take you to
where she be" and he does, some fucking
hellhole way over the east end of 14th
Street and up some chicken littered stairs,
but when we got to the top with him behind
me, he points to a door and before he can
say anymore I turn and kick him in the
face with everything I've got and he goes
down the stairs to the bottom coming up
screaming "You crazy motherfucker" and me
just begging him to come back for more
but he runs away and I open her door and
it ain't no bigger than a walk-in closet,
in fact I can see that's what it is,
converted to a "room" with a cot-size bed
and in it someone lies breathing deeply——
I can't see but I know it's her by the
smell I can never forget——as quietly as

I can I slip in beside her, touch her hair,
her face, her skin—it's hot, she's sick
with more than bad choices and hopeless
nights and whatever she's been through
since our last fight when I ran away to
the Air Force—I take her in my arms and
she opens her eyes and even in the darkness
I can see that glow as I say "It's me"
and she says "I know" and adds "don't fuck
me, I'm sick" and I say "No, no, no, no,
no, baby, I'm not here to fuck you, I'm here
to take care of you" and she gets as close
to crying as I've ever seen her or she's
ever seen me, she says "I just didn't want
you to get it too"—and all I can say is
"God how I still love you" and God how I
still do, sitting there in the bar with
Pauline and her, as she thanks me for
rescuing her that time saying she owes me
so much as she remembers how the next
morning we were woke up by the landlord
banging on the door—I don't tell her I
was already awake, staying up all night
holding her tight as she slept, watching
the light as it crept through the dirty
little window and over her skin and the
cigarette burn put there by a man I wish
I could find so I take it out on the
landlord as I open the door and he demands
his ten bucks for the week and I go
after him to kick in his fucking head
but he's already fled yelling about
the police so I know I got to get her
out of there—I help her into the one dress

she's got to wear, everything else long
since pawned or stolen, and I carry her
down the stairs and over to a friend's
apartment near Washington Square, where
we can stay on the couch and day after
day I feed her and bathe her and slowly
she responds until one night, just goofing
with her I make her laugh, and it's like
that scene in the story of Thomas Edison
when they turn on all the streetlights
at once for the first time in Manhattan—
that's the way it felt in my heart—so
here we are in this bar almost 30 years
later and she's thanking me for my part
in all that and Pauline's talking about
Big Brown who used to put me down for
being with a black girl, but who she liked,
cause he treated her right when he could
have killed her, and the time he got hit
with a butcher knife and The Duchess who
acted so cold, but once when I was roaming
around on my own without any home and the
bartender at Obie's wouldn't give me a
drink or a smoke, he suddenly changed his
mind and laid down my brand, Pall Mall,
and a shot of my favorite J.W. Dant and
pointed at The Duchess but when I started
to thank her she turned away the same way
Ralphie the Junkie did even though I was
gonna kick his ass for selling me soap
powder once, he saw me and Bambi were
really hungry one time and took us to what
seemed like a pretty fancy joint back
then, not much more than a Howard Johnson's

and bought us dinner and desert and
threw in a lady's magazine for Bambi and
when I started to say thanks he went
"Fuck that" and walked away leaving us
standing there feeling light as the air
so happy not to be hungry anymore—oh
man, when I open up that door to those
days sometimes I think it was all a dream,
something I made up to seem tough to
later friends, but shit, there I was
last Friday night sitting with these two
grandmothers, one still acting tough but
so happy we're all together she can't stop
smiling and the other still acting crazy
but it doesn't scare me anymore or make
me mad, it makes me laugh and tell her how
cute she is and she says "Cute is
inappropriate for a 35-year-old woman"
and I say "Bambi, you're 46"—she says
"37, that's it"—I take her face in my hands
and say "Hey, I owe you so much too—"
and I realize I'm saying exactly what I
mean now because I am the man I was trying
to be back then when I was too high and
too young and too scared and too overwhelmed
by the feelings I had inside that made me
want to hide inside her eyes forever—
and right there in that bar with all those
people who don't know and could never
imagine the history of her and me—we kiss
and her lips are the same as they were
like the taste and the touch of home that
I tried to describe in all the poems I
wrote for years to her—but all I can

say when we finally pull away is "Hey,
I don't care how many husbands and wives
we've both had, you'll always be my woman"
—and she says "I'm glad" and it feels
so fucking great not to have to be bad or
hate half the world and scared of the rest
just because the best thing I knew when
I was 18 was the love I felt for the
beautiful crazy queen of all the lost souls
in our little New York street scene—hey
none of them became artists or songwriters
or famous or real estate brokers or rich—
a lot are dead or even more lost or sick—
sometimes when I'm in the city and I see
a familiar face on a gray-bearded black man
digging in the garbage, I think is that—?
but last Friday night at least three of us
were still alright, and together again—
can you dig how far I've come since then?
and I ain't talkin' about Hollywood.

SPORTS HEROES, COPS, AND LACE

Jackie Robinson was my first real sports hero,
my first real hero period.
My father once took me to see Jersey Joe Walcott
work out for one of his fights.
It was in a summer camp in the North Jersey hills.
We called them mountains back then.
Jersey Joe was already getting old, but he was game
and carried himself like a champ.
I even got introduced to him by my father's friend,
and I remember how nice he was.
In fact I was struck by it, by his openness and
friendliness and unexpected gentleness
when it was obvious he could have easily killed
anybody there with his bare hands
if he felt like it. My father was a sporting man.
He played the ponies every day
and knew everybody at the track and even made a
little book on the side.
We always watched the Friday night fights together
on the old console black-and-white TV.
The Gillette song and that announcer with the high
nasal voice and my father
leaning out of his chair, already an old man to me,
but sporty, with what seemed
like closets full of sporting shoes and sport coats
and even a camel's hair overcoat
I used to sneak a feel of every time I went into the hall
closet. He'd point out Jake Lamotta,
call him "the possum" because he could play dead,
let a man batter him for what seemed
like hours, and then when the opponent dropped his guard

tear him apart. He had heart, it was said.
But all these guys seemed somehow tarnished to me, even Jersey
Joe. They were like my father's friends,
nice enough guys, who always treated me right, even if
I hated that they called me "little Jimmy."
I'd tell them my name is Michael
so then they'd call me Mikey, but they were okay.
Even the ones who were obvious bums
like Boots and Mary, and Frenchy, and all these characters
my father had grown up with and run
with and continued to help out till the day he died.
It was like living inside a
Damon Runyon story, and I dug the romance of it,
because despite the idea people
usually have who have never lived that life, it *is* romantic,
in fact, that's one of the appeals
of that world, any kind of underworld, the bookies
the petty crooks and over-the-hill
champs, there was a glamour and
a romance there, even with the old bags and bums like
Boots and Mary, hey, I used to see
them holding hands as they searched the ground for butts.
But it wasn't until Jackie Robinson
entered the big leagues that I found a hero of my own.
The man had something more than the romance
of the streets and sporting life and my father's friends
and closets of my home. The man had what
my father feared and desired most—"class"—the thing
my father's friends would toast him for.
And it was true that in our neighborhood my father had
some class and carried it as best he could.
But in the face of people more comfortable in this world
and self-assured, my father would get
awful humble, and almost do a kind of white man shuffle

that made me feel that maybe I wasn't
good enough either. He'd pretend that we were better off
where we were and among our own kind,
and we all grew up believing the other Americans, the ones
whose families had been here for a long time,
whose kids went to college and whose fathers and uncles
ran the businesses that really mattered—
we were taught they weren't as happy as we thought we were,
especially when we partied or married or
someone died. But inside, I knew it wasn't pride, it was
some unacknowledged form of ambition suicide.
Don't think beyond these streets, these ways of being or
you might get hurt. We knew our place.
And then Jackie Robinson entered major league baseball as the
first of his race, and I saw a kind of
dignity in the face of the obscenities that greeted him
every day on the field and it made my chest
swell with pride, which didn't make any sense since I was
obviously white and knew nothing about
this man except that he could stand up to the lowest forms
of hatred and not let it affect him,
at least not in any way I could see. And I saw a model for me,
when the kids would do the cruel things
kids can sometimes do, I would think of Jackie Robinson and I
would try to be heroic like him,
and sometimes it worked. Even when they called me a jerk
and a race traitor and all the rest,
because when we played stickball and each took on the persona
of our favorite players, I would
pick him, and the other white guys would berate me and try to
get me to react the way I usually did,
with my fists or my murder mouth or something that could be
turned to their amusement as long as
I was out of control. But when I took on his name for the game,

I took on his dignity too, and it
got me through their petty prejudices and opened up a whole new
world. Sometimes it even worked with
the girls. Until they too began to feel compelled to make
fun of one of their race who was inspired
by a man whose face was handsome and intense but happened
to be denser in its reflection of the sun
than one of us. Jackie Robinson was the guide to the
outside world for me, his example let me see
that what I was taught was not necessarily true, and what I
always suspected I knew might be. He gave
me a way to go beyond that world and to go deeper into me—
and when I came back, what I had learned
helped me to see that even the people I had left behind knew
these things too. When my cop brother
and my cop brother-in-law and my cop uncle and cousin and
boarder in my mother's house denounced
the riots in the '60s always in racist tones, I'd confront
them about the black friends they often
had in their homes and they would say, that's different,
that's L.J., he's my friend, he's not one
of them. Or when I'd point out how they often dressed and
spoke and drove the same cars and hung
out in the same bars and all the rest, they'd get hurt like
I had turned into some kind of foreigner,
one of those old-time Americans who didn't understand and
tried to grandstand with their liberal ideas
when they lived in wealthy suburbs and never had to deal
with the reality of our streets. They'd tell
me they didn't think they'd ever meet one of their own kind
as blind to what was real as me and then
they'd try and make me see that they didn't haven't anything
against the Jews and blacks and Italians
and homos and even the rich, because they all had friends or

even in-laws that fit those labels,
they'd try to tell me it's about being true to who you really are
no matter how far your people have come
or haven't come, and then they'd tell some story about how
it used to be and then they'd ask me
how come I never wrote those Damon Runyon stories about them
or more importantly about my father—
they figured I didn't bother because I got too far away
from what I'd been—when I moved
away from the old neighborhood after my father said I was
no good for wanting to marry a
black girl and having too many black friends—and then,
when I finally came back again,
so many years after I left him—this time we didn't
fight—because I asked him about
Boots and Mary, whatever happened to Louis the Lip or
Two Ton Tony—he talked all night
& it finally felt alright with him—he talked about how
his mother had been a "live-out maid"
when he was a kid—we never talked about politics or the
division that had driven us all into
fear and insecurity—I listened, he talked, and after I
left he called me up & asked if I had
enough to get my kids Xmas presents this year—I said I
did—I never took a dime from him
before, why should I start now—one of my sisters called
and told me because it was the only way
he could say I love you—so I called him back & said hey,
I could use two hundred & he said
it's yours—& I took the kids to see him with the
gifts his money made possible—
he was watching sports on the TV—and all of a sudden he
brought up Jackie Robinson—
how he always admired that man's dignity & a few days later

he called up the only brother he
had left and told him to take him to the hospital—
the doctor called my sister &
told her there's nothing we can find, we'll keep him
overnight and send him home—
& of course he died & this time when they tried to bring him
back he refused—hey, I don't know
why he wanted to die—that was a lot of years ago—all I
know is when I saw *Field of Dreams*
I started to cry—I didn't even know why—my father and
I never even tried to play any game—
but hey you know I'm not ashamed to carry his name—I hope
he feels the same.

TRICK OR TREAT

growing up in the Catholic faith
we knew all about the true meaning
of Halloween—All Souls' Day and
All Saints' Day were real important
to all of us, because all of us had
family that had already passed, and
as much as we knew we wanted the
ones we left behind praying for us
is how much we prayed for the ones
already gone—of course that didn't
mean we didn't get into mischief—
in fact, in Jersey in the 1950s we
had a week-long buildup to Halloween—
it started lighthearted with chalk
night, although we could come up
with some pretty innovative things
to do with chalk—I remember drawing
a white line across the black asphalt
and then two of us would sit on opposite
curbs and when a car was speeding about
ten feet away we'd reach down as though
we were grabbing the ends of the white
line to yank up some kind of rope barrier
and the driver would hit the brakes and
screech to a halt as we ran laughing back
into the darkness of allies and backyards—
and there was soap night—mostly writing
washable graffiti all over peoples windows
and cars, sometimes it got a little scary
when somebody would put a swastika on a
car and it would turn out to belong to a

Jewish family that would call the cops and
the papers would report an outburst of
anti-Semitism when we didn't even know
what the word meant or who owned the car
anymore than we dug Nazis, some of us had
lost fathers and brothers to the Nazis
but still—their symbols and rituals
were somehow cool and hard not to play
around with, just like fire—we didn't
have a fire night like they do in Detroit
now, but on the night before Halloween, after
nights of a kind of playful mischief, we
had to get into the real thing—this was
officially known as mischief night, and
every year someone fell for the burning
bag of dogshit bit—you know, find the
dogshit, get a paper bag, then somebody
had to put the dogshit in the bag—big
points for acting like that was no big deal,
then pick the house of the biggest pain
in the ass in the neighborhood and sneak
onto his porch, light the bag and ring
the doorbell, then run like hell and laugh
your ass off from the shadows as he opens
the door, sees the burning bag, and starts
stamping on it to put it out, getting
rapidly softening dogshit all over his shoes,
his porch, hopefully everything in sight—
but that wasn't the only trick we had on
mischief night—we'd remove stop signs—
exchange street signs, jack up the backs
of cars just enough to look normal but not
go anywhere when the owner stepped on the
gas, hell, we'd wander into strange neighbor-

hoods, get lost in fantasies of really big
pranks, some that wouldn't pay off for days,
weeks, months, years, like switching not just
street signs, but babies, headlines on news-
papers, seeds in backyard gardens, ideas
of who we might be someday—until some
of the older guys would get bored and start
drifting away to secret schemes we little
kids could only dream of, but we all agreed
on one thing, no self-respecting little thug
would dress up in any costume the next night—
we'd trick or treat alright—by going into
the candy stores and bowling alleys and hangouts
of the neighborhood to hit the owners up for
cash or cigarettes or cigarillos or maybe
we'd accept some candy if it was tough enough,
like jawbreakers or rum-flavored chocolate
cherries, and we'd browse through all the
girlie magazines we felt like that night
and the owner would know enough not to even
think of trying to stop us or he'd wake up
to find his gum machine on his roof or his
sign altered from ESSEX SWEETSHOP to SEX WOP
and old Shell Shocked Sam who owned the candy
store that one of my uncles supposedly crawled
to just before he died when he shot himself by
accident just trying to impress my aunt that he
really could take his life if he felt like it—
Sam would jump around in that St. Vitus'
dance of his and promise us anything, just
to keep us from pulling any of the stunts
we pulled anyway over the years, until not
only his fears but all of ours were realized
one trick or treat night when two guys from

the neighborhood nobody would ever fight
with, not even my brother or brother-in-law,
the cops, even though these guys were
only 16 and 17 they had a reputation
for being able to cream anyone who tried to
fuck with them, but high on something more
than the cough medicine or bennies or what-
ever goofballs we had access to, these two
cut loose one Halloween night in the A&P at
the bottom of my street, the one where
my cousin who got stabbed had to work when
they threw him out of tenth grade for
getting a ninth-grader pregnant, threw her
out too, and just to let you know, they
got married and had five kids and another
one who ran away from his family to join
theirs and legally changed his name to
Lally when he was 21, and they all are good
people today, with their own families & homes
that they work hard for, and until their
mother died a few years ago, my cousin and
her were as tight as that night when he
got stabbed but wouldn't tell the cops
who did it—as tight as these other two
guys were when they got high and broke
into the A&P 'cause they wouldn't give
them any liquor when we tried to trick or
treat them earlier, and when the cops
found them they couldn't understand how
they let themselves get caught—they
were laughing and giggling, laying in
the aisles, pounding the floor and there
was white bread and baloney, every last
bit the store had, thrown everywhere so

it was even hanging from the lights—
and they were laughing so hard they
were crying as the cops took them away
and all you could hear them say was
"we forgot the fucking ketchup"—so
I guess you know what's coming—they
ended up doing time as it turned out for
some sort of early primitive credit card
scheme they had going through some rich
girls they were diddling, and the next
year, while they were still away, after
the A&P closed down for the day, and
there was nobody around, some little
burgeoning wise guys stole a case of
ketchup and doused the entire building
in commemoration of the neighborhood
toughs who had paved the way for the rest
of us to have our day of paying back the
world for all its fucked-up rules and
regulations that tried to keep us in our
place as though to reach out for something
more than an early marriage and a steady
job or try and change some things they
thought were good but we found stupid
would disgrace our families and our
whole fucking neighborhood—but I
decided to do it anyway, to try and
get away to where it wouldn't matter
what color or how many the women you
ended up living with or marrying might
happen to be—and they stayed there
until things got so bad they had to
move too—'cause on Halloween night now
they don't even go out for fear of

being stabbed or shot like so many
other places we can name—and still
the big boys at the top keep acting and
talking like it's still the same old
game, and maybe it is, 'cause they
still seem to be able to send the kids
off to fight and die for whatever they
say is right—and if you don't like
it and want to get funny or try and fight
it, they'll take care of you too—
without even saying boo—

HOLIDAY HELL

I always worked on Christmas. Well
not always, since I was about 13.
My father had this home maintenance
business, which meant we cleaned up
after rich people and fixed things in
their homes. There was always a lot
to do around Christmas, including
selling trees out in front of the
little hole-in-the-wall storefront.
We had this one special customer who
got this special fifty-foot tree every
year. On Christmas Eve, after his kids
went to bed, my brother-in-law the cop
Joe Glosh (short for Gloshinski) and me
would drive up with the tree and put it
up in the middle of this swirling kind of
Hollywood staircase, wiring it to the
banister here and there until we got it
steady and solid, ready for the silver
dollar tip we always got. My brother-
in-law would always wonder why the best
tree we ever saw always went to a Jew who
didn't even believe in Christmas, right?
Then he'd drop me back at the store and
go home while I waited there alone just
in case somebody might be waiting till the
last minute to buy a tree. Usually no one
was, and when it turned midnight I could
call the local orphanage and they'd come
by for whatever we had left, which my
old man would let me give them for free, and

then I could walk or hitchhike the few miles home. When we were little my sisters and I would exchange our gifts before we fell asleep, because we all lived in the attic together. The coolest thing was waking in the morning with this sound, like crunchy paper, and realizing it was our stockings at the foot of the beds that my ma had always somehow got up there without us catching her, and we'd get to open up all our stocking stuff before we woke the rest of the folks, our other brothers and grand-mother and the border, Jack, and our mom and dad. Then we'd all open stuff and go to Mass and come home for the big dinner. But by the time I got the attic to myself, 'cause my brother-in-law and that sister got a place of their own and my other sister joined the nunnery for a while, I got to working for the parks department too, because my old man didn't pay me, figuring I worked for room and board, so I had these other jobs, and the parks department had a busy day on Christmas 'cause all these kids would come down to the park to try their new sleds or skates, and I worked either on the hill or on the pond as a sort of guard and coach and general alarm man. I used to love seeing a wreck on the hill so I could slide down the snow on my engineer boots, the kind motorcycle dudes wear now, showing off my teenaged skill and balance for the teenaged girls who might be watching. I don't remember ever falling down, it was

something I was totally confident about. Now
that I think about it, I guess working on
Christmas wasn't so bad, even though I always
kind of felt sad anyway, especially after I
started dating black girls and knew I couldn't
take them home or share the holidays much
with them. But there was always something sad
about Christmas anyway, once you were over five
or maybe ten, how could it ever live up to your
expectations again? I also dug being a
working guy though, you know? Even today
when I see young working guys going by in
the backs of pickup trucks I catch their eye
and feel like I know what's going through
their heads, because of what was going
through mine, which was, any time now I'll be
out of this, a big star or wheeler dealer or
intellectual or anything that means a kind of
success you couldn't guess when you look at
me here under these conditions, 'cause now,
I'm a mystery to you, you don't know who I
am, you think you can categorize me but you
got no idea who I might be someday, or the
the richness of the life I live inside, and
you'll never know what it's like to be as
cool as I sometimes feel when you look at me
and see a guy from some kind of ethnic mystery
you can't comprehend except in the most simplistic
terms, and who is so free he can work in public
and get dirty and sweat and wear his hair greasy
and his tee shirt rolled and know you would never
mess with him unless you're a woman and get a whim
to find out what it's like to give a piece of ass
to someone from the working class—I dug the

kind of coolness of it, of knowing I was a lot more
than these ordinary citizens could comprehend,
that I could be sexy in ways their men were too
restrained to be, that I could be threatening in
ways their men would be too frightened to be, that
I could get down and dirty and not give a fuck
what I looked like in public, even though I knew
I looked cool, that I could be inside a life and
world they could never even guess the intensity and
romanticism and pure exhilaration of because it
didn't depend on material goods and worldly
success but on loyalty and honesty and standing
up for yourself and all the rest of your kind
when you were put to the test—hell I used to
love looking back into their eyes and thinking
someday they'll be so surprised to find out
what was going on in my head when I put it in
a book or on film or tell them about it in their
bed—so even though I came home late for the
big dinner and my fingers and toes all froze
'cause guys like us could never make a fuss about
the cold by wearing scarves or gloves or any of
that rich kid stuff, and maybe I'd get a little
drunk when nobody was looking and try to get the
phone into the closet or somewhere where I could
be alone for a few minutes to call some girl
they might call colored and wrong, and end up
later that night sleeping on the floor of the
kitchen with the new puppy so he wouldn't keep
everyone awake with his scared yelps and in the
morning scandalize my grandmother when she found
me in my boxer shorts the puppy asleep on my
chest and she'd rouse me and make me get dressed
but not without telling me I was just like my

father, I didn't have any ashes, which was her
way of implying I didn't have any ass to speak
of, and then I'd help her get her stockings over
her crippled legs and have something to eat and
go to work again, maybe this time on the pond,
where I'd get to slide across the ice to rescue
stumbling teenaged girls while "Earth Angel" or
"Blue Christmas" blared over the loudspeakers
and in my heart, knowing for sure I was going
to be a part of some important history, and I
was—and still am.

20 YEARS AGO TODAY

We were a couple of kids
with a kid—weren't we Lee—
ever since this topic came up
I've been thinking about you—
but not like I usually do,
I've been remembering what it was
that kept us together, the glue
that made it look to others
like our marriage worked—
I used to think it was the anger & sex—
I never talked much about love
I guess—and
after all the experience since us
all the lovers and living together
being married and being in a "relationship"
the flirtations and infatuations
the romances and affairs and rolls
in the hay and pokes and fucks and
fantasies, what do I know about it Lee?
I went out with a woman last week,
intelligent, accomplished, attractive,
a great body, like yours only harder,
that's the way most of them are now,
at least out here, they all work out so much,
but this one does it with ballet,
you'd have dug that too, but she's
taller than you, she could actually do
it if she wasn't already successful
at something else not quite so demanding
or deforming—anyway, we had a nice enough
time, but she's still in love with somebody

else and I guess I am—or was—too—
but that never stopped me with you,
even though you knew—
I remember how understanding you were about that
before we got married, but then after
you said if you ever saw her on the street
you'd cut out her heart and I believed you would
—back then it somehow seemed good
to be with someone that passionate and crazy,
both of us acting so lower class city street tough
as though we weren't just a couple of kids
afraid the world might really be too rough
for us after all, what did we know heh?
anyways, those were the days Lee—
things hadn't gone all wrong,
we were still getting along—
making love every night,
and I don't think we'd begun to fight yet—
like about John Lennon leaving his wife—
something you were sure I was going to do to you
when I became that successful too, which
everyone seemed to think was inevitable back then—
well, not everything we thought would happen came
true—at least not for me & you—
remember how all those predictions about me
always ended with "if he lives that long"—
every time I got in my old telephone van and turned
the key, I had to take this deep breath first,
then curse the right-wing assholes who sent me
death threats in the mail, with pictures
of crosshairs aimed at the back of my neck,
or descriptions of my van blowing up or my
house burning down—those guys
probably went on to work for Reagan and

Bush & Quayle, but that's a whole
other story you don't want to know about—
what I'm trying to get out now is the fact
that I hardly ever write about you and me Lee
and all those years we spent together—
and of all that time, maybe February 1969 was the
highlight, you were still jealous of everyone
but they didn't have you on the run and never
would—and I was really being good—you know
I never cheated on you, not once in all those
early years, despite your fears and mine—
even that time that girl said I had with her,
I don't know what that was about, maybe just
that I was in the papers a lot then and she
somehow wanted to be a part of that—what do
I know Lee, I got girls younger than our
daughter after me now and it's just because
they want to read their poetry at Helena's—
I don't even want to get into that either—
hey, Lee, what I'm remembering is a night so cold we
have to wrap our baby in her little snowsuit
to sleep in, 'cause all we got is this one little
oil stove in the middle of the Quonset hut
we were living in, yeah, the kind with the
ruffled corrugated tin in a semicircle—
so what little heat there was hovered
over our heads in the very middle of the house,
the only place I could stand straight up anyway—
I remember the water in the diaper pail had a thin
layer of ice on it in the morning, but that
night, we got naked under tons of covers and
those old quilts you dug so much, reminding you
of your mother's country roots, we were
probably high on some reefer as usual—

and I was probably tired from my three part-time
jobs and all the classes I took to get through
school quick before I hit one of those smug
professors or graduate student assistants—
I think I already quit teaching at the Free
University, my class on Stalin, not because
I dug him, but because if people were gonna
talk about him I figured they oughta know
what he did and said and wrote or had ghostwritten
for him, but when Russia invaded Czechoslovakia, I
gave up caring about any of those Communist
thugs and their theories—and I had already
lost the election for Sheriff of the County,
despite the great letters and support I got—
I did pretty good actually, a lot better
than Hunter Thompson did the following year
when *Rolling Stone* tried to pretend he was
the first stoned-out writer to run for sheriff
anywhere—but that's another story too—
what I'm remembering is that old brass bed
you dug so much, and us in some kind of
clutch under all the stuff, we could see
our breath in the dark night air it was
so cold—there was a lot of snow on the ground
as usual, but that was out there through
those tiny windows, the dark Iowa sky and
the stars, and the way they looked through
our stoned hallucinations, your fears about
what all my revolutionary commitments might
mean, where we would go, what scene we would
get enmeshed in next, none of that had come
up yet, this was a pause just before we
got ready to move on to the next and toughest
part of our time together—now, we were still

able to weather all the shit we had been through
and still stay together, and we knew how to
do that so well in bed Lee—goddamn it, it
got so confusing later, didn't it? but we knew—
feminists tried to tell me in later days that
you were probably faking those perfect orgasms
but what the fuck did they know? we were kids
who learned how to make love together—
sure we'd been around when we met, so much more
than most in those days too, but we knew
what didn't work and what did, and we taught each
other, and we got to a place where every night
after we turned out the light and turned to each
other under those covers we could make everything
good for a little while, we could make each other
feel like we'd just discovered the secret of life,
like we truly understood the reason anyone could
take pride in words like *husband* and *wife,* and
yeah I still had a lot more to learn,
but honey, we had enough sensual
power between us those nights to burn that Quonset
hut down if we'd wanted to, but all we wanted to
do was become one, and we did, good enough that
night 20 years ago to create a son,
and a beautiful boy he is Lee—you'd be proud of him—
as you would of our daughter—as I truly was of you—
standing up to the geeks and assholes who wanted
to know what happened to your face or wanted you
to replace it with a plastic one—I never understood
completely your reasons for leaving it the way it was
but I also never gave a shit Lee, I respected you
and I believe you respected me, and you know,
I think that's what it was that made it last as long
as it did, and that made it possible for us every

night to reach that same sensual height
at the same time together—goddamn it kid, we
knew what we were doing in bed, no matter what
anybody later said—I grew to sometimes hate you
Lee, and some of the things you said to suit
those later feminist days, but hey, you never revised
that part about us in bed, and neither did I,
no matter what other kinds of things I might
have said about you—
you were my love, my little darling in that bed,
and I was your man, your boy, your loving friend—
we didn't have the fancy moves I learned later—and
maybe that was just as well, we just did what came
so naturally and felt so goddamn swell—
yeah I'm still throwing in those really dumb rhymes
from the old days of toasting & dirty dozens—
aw Lee, Lee, Lee, when our daughter came to
live with me, I used to see you in her sometimes
and it would get me mad—it was always the stuff
that made me leave you finally like you always
predicted, only not because I was some great success,
but because there was no more room for those sweet
nights under all that feminist duress, and because
I wanted to finally see what it might be like with
some other bodies I guess—and I did, it has been
sometimes really great and amazing and even
now and then full of love and grace, but you know,
now sometimes when I look at our daughter's
face, I see you still, only not what I grew to feel
bad about, there was a sweetness in those days Lee,
to those kids with their kid we used to be and
especially 20 years ago tonight when we created
another one, I see you too in him, our son—I'm
sorry it didn't work out, and I can't even express

how bad I feel about what happened to you, at least I
don't feel guilty about it anymore, because I've learned
that guilt is just pride in reverse, taking credit for
things you have no control over—and I had no control
over that fucked-up operation and those six years in
whatever state you were in inside that comatose body—
but you were always afraid I wouldn't be able to take
care of the kids, after the years of poverty and
crazy Irish irresponsibility, at least it seemed that
way to you—so now the kids are taken care of—
thanks to lawyers and malpractice suits and it's
all way out of my hands—and here I am Lee—thinking
of you and how strong you were for such a tiny lady—
and how you always knew something the rest of us
didn't—I wonder if you knew then that I loved you, and
just didn't know it, except when I would show it in bed—
and no matter what went on in my head later or does
now about me and you—I guess it's about time I
admitted I still do.

DISCO POETRY

I remember where I was when
JFK got assassinated, when
Martin Luther King got shot,
when the first man walked on
the moon, when Elvis died,
when John Lennon was killed,
and when I first heard Barry
White—I was in a record
store in a black neighborhood
of Washington DC, known on
those streets as Chocolate City
—a young handsome platform-
shoed extroverted gay black man
was talking to the clerk about
what he had just discovered on
a trip to New York and when he
said "Barry White" the clerk says
"we just got it in today" and he puts
on "I'm Under the Influence of Love"
and the album sold out in the next
few minutes. Everyone in the store
bought it, including me, the only
white, but also in platform shoes—
now why does that seem so tacky and
shallow and all the negative adjectives
just the simple word "disco" seems to
conjure up these days, unlike say "rock"
—I remember when I first heard Janis
Joplin, it was at a party in a
farmhouse rented by some University
of Iowa students, I walked in, pretty

high, and got higher when I heard
her blasting her version of "Summertime"
into the black rural night as George
K. shot some Adrenalin, he said—
that he had copped from a hospital—
directly into his chest and then slammed
to the floor and shook violently while his
one real eye rolled back and his skin turned
a whiter shade of pale and several of
us long-haired guys picked him up and
walked him around outside for over an hour
until we were sure he wasn't going to die
and then we came back in and did our own drugs
and danced and forgot where we were or
who we were or anything else about that
night except George almost OD'ing and
Janis singing "take a, take another little
piece of my heart now" well now, how can anyone
compare that kind of thrill, or the first
time we saw Elvis on TV or The Beatles coming
to America with fucking disco—come on man,
Travolta in that sappy low-rent white suit and
low-rent white flick, shit, disco was black
music first, emphasizing the bass beat, giving
birth to "rap" in a basic kind of way no rapper
would ever say, I'm sure, and then taking the tour
of the white world through the "gay" clubs first,
not through some Italian thugs in Brooklyn—
but still, where, outside of James T. Farrell's
Studs Lonigan, had we ever seen a more accurate
portrayal of the male ritual of getting dressed
to go out than in that scene in *Saturday Night
Fever*—and what else inspired Michael Jackson to
inspire us with some of his hippest stuff in

the lyrics and music of "Off the Wall," or got
an expatriate diva back from Europe, where her
soft porn sound gave birth to the Eurotrash
that followed, only to become the most powerful
and successful black woman of her time, Donna
Summers, who in her prime made us love to love
her bad girl moves and glamorize our need to
dance and summarize our post-war angst with
songs that satisfied our frenetic desire to
outlast the collective shame and confusion by
singing "I Will Survive" and how better to
do that than by just "oh-oh-oh-oh staying
alive"—yes, it was the '70s when the reality
of everything we had raved against for fear
it would come true did—so we partied like
being bored to death was a true possibility—
and rediscovered style with a relentlessness
that even made the '50s look like happy days—
the '50s that looked so lame in the '60s like
the '60s looked so lame in the '70s and the '70s
have looked so lame in the '80s—but it's
almost the '90s now, and if you want to be
on the cutting edge, just go back 20 years
and you'll be there—hey, in the '70s it
looked for a while like the Republicans
would never gain the presidency for the rest
of the century after what they did to us in
Vietnam and with Watergate and all the lies
and dirty tricks and secret wars that were
uncovered, the Democrats might be corrupt
but the Republicans were corrupt and
self-righteous, is there a more repulsive
combination than that? they're like blow-
dried Noriegas, and the '70s gave birth to

AIDS and the Bush conspiracies that led to
the power of people who continue to sell
this country and indeed the world out from
under us as we turned our backs on the
moral obligations we understood intuitively
only a few years before—hey, the '70s weren't
a bore or so bland and free of style as we
thought, in fact it might take a while but
if we start to relate what really went down,
we're gonna find out they're gonna come
around again to where we all can defend
the right to live a life of love instead of
greed and fear and constant reinterpretation
of the year we first heard Barry White—
& maybe we'll go out & dance all night or
maybe I mean talk or maybe I mean hold each
other like we are the light, me & you, & maybe
we'll make peace with ourselves & the rest
of the world again like disco once helped us do

FROM "OF"

the sound of police cars
& rain accumulating in
the light fixture in
the bathroom—the most
dangerous leak in the
house—like that time
in the loft in New
York on Duane Street
when my seven-year-
old son Miles yelled
for me—there was a
mouse running up my
mattress-on-the-floor bed
getting close to his head
as he watched the TV
& I took off my Doctor
Scholl's and squashed it
without even thinking
& he went on watching
TV without even blinking
& not too many
nights later I snuck in
a 22-year-old woman
after he went to sleep
and we made love for
hours and then laid there
thinking until she said—
"how old did you say you
were?" & I told her—38—
and she said "that's
amazing"—& I said,

wanting to hear her say how
good I was—how young I
looked—how whatever it was
that amazed her about my
being that age that time,
so I said "what's amazing
about it?" & she said "a
guy your age, still sleeping
on a mattress on the floor"

HAVING IT ALL

When I was a kid,
I had no doubt I would win world acclaim:
a Nobel Prize for my novels, plays, and poetry,
and be the first Nobel laureate to also win
an Oscar for writing, directing, and
starring in the world's most popular
movie in the history of film—
and all this after becoming the world's
most famous and successful singer and musician
who would destroy forever the boundaries
between rock 'n' roll and jazz and blues and
all forms of popular and esoteric music
with my enormous talent and universal appeal,
and of course I would accept the Nobel
while serving as the most effective
and most popular president of the USA
in its entire history—which naturally
would be merely a prelude to my accepting
the presidency of the world, united finally
as a direct result of the influence and impact
of my political theories.

This is all true.
I believed this,
and continued to believe it throughout my life.
In one way or another.
How could I help it?
When I saw James Dean trying to do what looked
like a way too self-conscious bad imitation
of the little juvenile delinquent I thought I was
or believed I understood firsthand at the time,

I knew in my heart that the truth I thought I saw
missing in his acting was present in me
every day of my life.
And when I saw Brando on his motorcycle
or Elvis on TV, I could see that these guys
had something, but how could it compare
with me? They were obviously pretending to be
something I knew I really was.
Their sexuality was like a game they were playing,
but my sexuality was no game to me,
I could spend eternity in hell for what I was feeling,
and the only thing that kept me from reeling
my way into an institution, which was where
they put lower-middle-class teenagers with too much
passion then, the only thing that prevented that
was the revelation that what I was feeling was
not only not a sin, but in fact an assignment from God:
to show the world how to love, again.

Now maybe that was just an Irish-Catholic kid's
way of getting around sin,
but I believed it with all my heart
and knew it was true,
and was sure that the world would see that too,
when they finally put me on film or TV,
or stuck me on a stage with a band behind me.
I had no doubts about it,
I didn't even think I had to put any effort into it,
really, though when it came my way
I did learn how to play some instruments
and did get up on stages and perform
or talk or walk around and let the inspiration
come out of me in words I found profound,
if nobody else did. I truly felt

I had a mission no less ambitious
than to embody love so perfectly
in all I did that the people of the world
would finally let go of all their fears about each
other and we could all just be ourselves at last
and leave everyone else alone to be themselves—
or maybe help them out if they needed it,
because we might need it sometime too,
you know, all that stuff that people did
get into for a while in the '60s in ways
I thought were somehow my doing—I mean,
I took myself so seriously I got proprietary
about almost everything I dug—
I wasn't totally out of control,
I never thought I was responsible for
athletic events or minor wars or stuff
I cared about but not that much—
but almost every hip style since I was a kid
I thought at least in part could not have
evolved if somehow someone hadn't picked up
on what I was wearing and doing—
yeah, all that ego stuff,
that obvious covering up
for the insecurity and fear
that maybe I wasn't enough—
but come on now, tell the truth,
didn't you feel that way too,
couldn't you see how obviously
inferior the supposedly great leaders
were, or even the great thinkers,
when you read Marx and Lenin and Jefferson and
Neitzsche and Kierkegaard and Wittgenstein and
St. Thomas, and Sartre and Hemingway and Stein,
didn't you really feel, as I certainly did,

that the truth was still being hidden away,
as if they really didn't know what it was
or were too afraid to say—
yeah, like I said, I felt that way,
until just the other day,
like sure I coulda been bigger than Elvis
or Marlon or JFK, only, you know, nobody asked
me to make a record or star in their movie or
run for president on their ticket—
well, actually, I did get asked to
be on a record with other New York
poets and performers once, like Laurie
Anderson, who looked like a hippie then,
but then she got her hair cut and spiked it
and dyed it and started wearing makeup
that accentuated her eyes and more or less
doing a female version of my style back then
and you know the rest—and people did
ask me to star in their movies, like the
one where I got to be the hero and stick
a wooden stake into a bald Dracula on
a farm in South Jersey, and when I took
my son to see the blown-up poster of me
doing just that on 42nd Street, he said
"gee dad, it looks like you're
killing some bum with a broom handle—"
and I once did run for office, sheriff
of Johnson County Iowa on the Peace and
Freedom ticket, Eldridge Cleaver was our
candidate that year for president—
though I thought at the time I had a
better political perspective—
so yeah, I guess I've had my chances,
especially when I think of all the

romances I've had with the women I
only dreamt about back then—only, when I
think about that mission I thought I was on,
I see that I turned it all into sexuality
that was all about how I could satisfy me
even when I did that by satisfying you
because that made me feel like I was still
being true to my assignment from God,
and who knows? maybe I was—

The truth is, I did all the things
I once dreamed I would, but either they didn't
turn out so good or what I fantasized they'd be
or it was me who didn't pull it off,
not prepared or just not good enough—
and when I finally accepted that
not too long ago, instead of feeling bad,
I felt this inner glow of peace and relief,
like I could finally get to know myself
without the pressure of being Elvis/Marlon/
JFK/Beckett/Kerouac/Dylan/Lennon/and the
rest, I didn't have to prove to myself
or anyone else anymore that I was the best
and just got overlooked somehow, I didn't
even have to save the world without your
help, being love and all that, all I had
to do was listen to my heart and not my ego
and tell the truth with whatever language
is truly mine and be of service in any way
I can and just go ahead and be the man I am—

2

I'M AFRAID I'M GONNA START CRYING

(& OTHER LOVE POEMS)

SOMETHING BACK

I never had a backache before
I started working out,
now I'm like all those other
jock Adonises, pretending to be
the healthiest man you've ever
scanned when it's all a sham—
I can't even stand up straight
anymore, or pick something
up off the floor without
making noises I used to hear
only the real old geezers make—
oh for heaven's sake, my mother
would say if she could hear me now
from wherever she went when I
watched the line go flat for
the last time, anyway, she'd say
oh for heaven's sake, don't make
yourself out to be so old when
you're my baby, the youngest of
the fold—who never had the chance
to hold her the way a grown man
can do, the way I hold my kids or
friends or other women or you—
but, that isn't really true,
because not too long ago, when
I was lying on my couch in the
middle of the afternoon, just
sort of digging the way the light
came through the trees and windows
in ways that spread these rays
all through the room, dispelling

any gloom I might have had and
reminding me of when I was four
or five and my mother told me
how each little speck of dust—
don't they call them mites?—was
actually an angel, which was enough
to keep me fascinated for days
in ways that probably led directly
to me being the kind of dreamer
who writes poems and lives on loans
and spends some afternoons just
lying on a couch mesmerized by a
certain slant of light and the way
it ignites a kind of heat in my
heart that starts the gratitude
flowing, when all of a sudden I
see my mother, kind of glowing
but very real, and without even
thinking I open my arms and take
her in my embrace in just that
way I never got the chance to,
like a grown man who knows what
it means to suffer and to be
comforted in the strength of
the arms of someone who loves you—
no, more than that, it is a thing
about feeling strong in a way
that still seems manly today,
I can't defend or even describe
this feeling right, but it was
there, in me, as I held my mom
in the afternoon light, so long
after she had gone for good and
then I looked and there my father

stood, weeping, and I knew without
thinking he was crying because
he felt left out and misunderstood
and I opened my arms to him,
because it was true I never got to
hold him that way either, with me
being the parent, the grown-up one
now, with me having been through
enough to forgive them for whatever
mistakes we all make, yeah, I just
never got to embrace these two
people whose love and devotion to
each other was so strong it lasted
a lifetime long, I remember them
holding hands on their couch as
they watched TV, like two teenagers,
and they were already old, having
had me by surprise at the end of
a brood of seven—what I'm
trying so hard to say is on that
day when they appeared to me I
really did see them standing there
in the golden air of the afternoon
light and I felt like I had the
chance to let them see I turned
out all right, and I didn't have
to cry about what has slipped away,
because I got something back.

YOUNG LOVE

When I was a kid I remember
going out with this girl
whose father ran a neighborhood
bar—he was known for his fits
of violence—one time when she
was talking to me on the phone
he came home and ripped the thing
out of the wall in the middle of
our conversation—I thought
she hung up on me and was kinda
hurt until she finally reached me
a few days later after everything
had quieted down—I remember
the first time I took her out,
they lived over the bar on the
border of Newark in a tough Irish-
Italian neighborhood that's now
a tough African-Puerto Rican one—
when I walked in she introduced
me to him, a big overgrown lummox,
the kind of Irish bully that made
me know why I wanted to get away
from that part of Jersey first
chance I got—and I did—but
back then I was still a kid with
nowhere to go that didn't end up
with me trying to sleep in the
snow—so, anyway, as I go
toward him sitting on the couch
to shake his hand the way I was
taught, he says "I thought she said

you played football" and I said
"I do" and he made some cutting
remark about how in his day someone
as thin and light as me woulda been
used for the football, and I said
something back about how maybe he'd
like to fucking try it sometime like
right now, and he looked like he
might and then laughed and said I was
alright but must have changed his mind
by the time he ripped the phone off
the wall—actually in that time and
place this girl was sort of classy
to even have a phone and a bar they
maybe didn't actually own but could
make at least the upstairs their home—
lots of girls I dated I had to call
their neighbors and ask them to run
next door or up the stairs to pass
some coded message on to them—
but this one girl was obviously
not thrilled to have a phone when
it came with the father she had—
but she didn't know what to do—
they didn't have books and seminars
and TV movies and newspaper stories
and anonymous meetings or much of
anything back then to tell a kid
what to do about fathers who drank
too much and then got violent—
we all knew about it, we all lived
with some version of it, and she
did what most of the kids I knew
did, she got cynical and tough—

so much that when we'd finally find
some quiet place under the stars
away from all the bars and the
anger they fed, we'd be doing some
heavy bodywork and then lay back
to look at the stars, and I could
never stop myself from going off
into them with my dreams of another
way—I'd start to sketch with
words the house we'd live in with
a fireplace we could lay in
front of like in movies I had seen
and in the morning we would walk
to the ocean nearby to say good
morning and watch the boats glide
by—this is true, I can see her
next to me on the ground as I let
my words take me away from all that
was around us, surrounded us, and
I can see her turn to me and shatter
everything I'd shared—she was just
trying to get me to see how all of
what I said was pure fantasy—I swear
I can still hear her saying "Michael,
you're such a dreamer, we're only
fifteen, we probably won't even know
each other in two years"—and I remember
my reply—"You're probably right but
so what? It makes it better, it
makes me want to kiss you even more
and hold you even tighter and feel
so fucking in love and happy I want
to cry, or fly away to those stars
up there forever, now what the fuck

is wrong with that? if it makes us
feel better and happier and more in
love?" But she wasn't going for it,
she had her own agenda and it didn't
include those kind of dreams, and it
seems she was right, because it wasn't
even two months before we were strangers
again—but in a way I was too, because
I live in that house with the fireplace
and the beach I say good morning to—
and if you're gonna lay down with me
in this quiet place I've finally found
and watch the fire with me and get up
in the morning to greet the nearby sea,
I want you to be as crazy about the
romantic possibilities as me—

ISN'T IT ROMANTIC?

She smiled when I passed her saying
"I love your poetry"
so naturally
I figured she
was just being polite
or thought that's what you're supposed to say
at these things or
was slightly high and caught my eye
and thought I expected a compliment
or didn't know what she was saying—
anything but just plain meaning it—
how could she mean it—
I hadn't even read yet
and she was the most beautiful woman in the place,
her face could sell me anything,
except my own worth,
for now—
that's how I felt about it—
and then I read—
and they wouldn't shut up—
not even when I told them
I was going to talk about their
pussies and assholes and cocks—
I could tell a few heard me and stopped talking
long enough to see if I meant it—
but pretty soon, they were filling the room
with their own chatter and it didn't seem to matter
what I read or said or—
so when I got down and walked across the floor
I wasn't expecting more compliments from anybody—
let alone her—

but there she was—still beautiful—
no, more so—her eyes still aglow with
what I still thought was fake or mock admiration—
so I just threw myself into dancing—
first with friends and then when they
disappeared, with myself—
through the crowd I could see her
dancing with her girlfriend
and when they whispered to each other and
looked over at me
I looked around to see what else
it might be—and sure enough, standing behind me was
a young dude who obviously
thought he was hot stuff,
like everyone else in the place in fact,
a room full of competing egos in black—
and when I turned back,
she was gone, so I closed my eyes
and disappeared into the music until
I had to open them or fall—
and when I did she was all I saw,
dancing now right there before me—
her girlfriend had moved over to my spot too—
and I thought for a minute, hey
maybe she does have some interest in me—
but then I see them both provoke
the hot-stuff dude into giving up his pose
to join them on the dance floor where I
can check him out up close—
he's not so hot—sure, he's got a lot of
hair and none of it's gray and it seems
to stay the way he planned it to, but hey,
when I was his age I looked more authentic
than that—hell, I still do—so does she—

maybe that's what she sees in me—and maybe
this hot-stuff guy is just shy and doesn't want to
show it—or blow it, the way I so often have—
and it makes him awkward in a kind of endearing way—
and suddenly hey, I can see that he's not anything more
than a friend—and he isn't dancing with her anyway—
because no matter how I try to misinterpret it,
she's obviously dancing with me, on purpose—
so I take the risk and smile at her,
and she smiles back—
and I can see I was wrong—
she isn't just beautiful, stunning, marvelous, and
incredibly naturally the girl of my oldest dream—
she doesn't seem crazy or needy or self-conscious or
aloof and full of hype like those model-slash-actress types—
she looks alright—and she's looking at me—
until I can't help but bite my tongue
to stop myself from screaming MARRY ME!!
what was I thinking? sure this was some cute kid
and maybe the dim lights hid my age
but when she sees me in the light—
might as well enjoy it—and I did—
and she made me forget all the rest—
especially when she leaned over and whispered in my ear
"What are you laughing at—is the dancing too much?"
"No" I shout back, afraid to get too near
for fear I'll just start sniffing at her skin
like a dog wanting to get in—
or let my lips just skim the surface of her
neck and chin and—
"I can never get too much dancing" I say—
"I'm just happy
because you're so beautiful"—
she smiles even more at that

and I feel great, and then she shouts back
"That was a beautiful poem you wrote about
the birthday girl—I'd love to have you write
a poem about me" and I don't miss a beat as my lips almost
meet her ear so she can hear me say "I'll
have to get to know you to do that"
and she says "I already know all about you"
and I try not to look like "oh no—shit—
what has she been told" as I ask "What
do you know?" and she says "That you have two kids
and are married" and I say "I got two kids
but their mother is dead" and she looks sad
for a minute and I'm thinking what the fuck
did you bring that up for at a time like this
in the middle of a dance floor when what
you really want to do is kiss this beautiful
apparition in this crowd of self-assured
white kids in black trying to be hip—
and I go on to say "In fact I'm living
alone for the first time in my life"
and that brings a smile to her face
and I want to get her out of this place
and into my arms where there aren't swarms
of kids who look like cleaned-up versions
of something I risked my life for and they
don't have to risk any more than a few hours
of possible boredom—so I say something
about leaving and getting something to eat
but getting her number first cause I'm really
thinking I got to go home and do some homework
if I want to do good tomorrow—while I'm also
thinking now that we're nearing more lights she'll probably
take flight and I can spend the rest of the night
feeling vindicated by my own sense of—

but that isn't what happened as we walked to the bar
and she told me we'd already met—
and I didn't remember, but she was right—
it was at one of the poetry nights
at Helena's, where she asked someone to
introduce her to me because she loved the way
I moved when I read my work and I'm
thinking I'll probably never move that way again
because already I'm trying to remember what I did—
and she's going on about how she came here tonight
just to see me and how maybe she should stop
and I'm saying "No, don't stop" and she's saying
"What are you gonna do, take me to lunch?"
and I say "No, dinner, are you hungry?"
and she says "I ate but you go fill your belly"
and there's nothing to do but leave,
I think, or buy her a drink, which she's
already doing, and I'm chewing on some
memory of what might be already as I
go home and try to leave a message on
her phone machine about how the soil
where she was born is probably blessed
from all the prayers of gratitude me
and all the rest of the guys she has
mesmerized have sent out there, and I'm thinking
of her hair, so dark and full and the way
it framed her face and those eyes that
sparkled and shone so bright even in
those dim lights and some female voice
answers the phone and I'm thinking, how did
she get home so fast? but it isn't her
and I can't leave my poetic message like that
so I try again the next day, only to hear the
same voice tell me she's still not there

and so I don't know what to do except leave my number
and then try and forget her because
I'm sure she'll never call, I'm sure I should have
taken her outside and kissed her until we choked
and then let her watch my smoke
as I hit the trail for my own busy life—
but I didn't, I left it like that—
me bumbling around for a way to say
hey I want to spend the rest of
my life seeing if you're who I think you are—
the star of my oldest dream,
the one about how if you really are honest
and good and true you get to fall in love
with someone who is falling for you
and it's the girl in the dream—the one
who seems like the most natural beauty on earth
and worth all the shit you've been through
to get to this place, where you can spend
the rest of your life looking at that face
and believing she wants to do the same with you—
only the phone keeps ringing and it's never her—
but you know what? the old ideas don't occur
to me this time, this time I feel like whatever
she doesn't do is okay—either way, I know
who I am and what I want, and what I do
is no longer based on what I can get from you—
but on what I can give as I live in a way
that will hopefully help us all get through each day
like it's the only one that counts now because it is.
Isn't *that* romantic?

THEY MUST BE GODS AND GODDESSES

Here's the deal, you make me feel
like a god come down from on high
to see how you humans get through
all the pain and heartaches life
and the world throws at you and yet
still continue to pass the tests
and overcome the obstacles and all
the rest we gods like to add to the
stew of your existence until you
give up and we can feel satisfied
that we really do have it better—
only watching you do the ordinary
human things a god would never stoop
to do, like cook and do the laundry
and unhook the VCR so you can hook up
the CD player again, I understand
why some men are constantly thanking
us for making them men, and I want to
be a man, so I can take your hand and
kiss it without feeling awkward, afraid
I might frighten you with the intensity
of my desire to pay homage to you, or
that you might misconstrue it to mean
I want you to do things with me I can't
even imagine now, let alone how it can
be done, this way you humans have of
becoming one with each other—I
watch you stir the sauce, or toss the
sheets into the dryer, or pick up a
child so effortlessly, and it is like
these gestures are higher than anything

a god can do for or against you—ever—
and I am in awe and want nothing more
than the chance to do these things too
the way I see you do, without pretension
or calculation, without restraint or
complaint, but with a kind of skill
that is a mystery to a god—there is a
will behind it that transcends the
merely habitual, the daily routine of
it, and transforms it into ritual as
precise and mysteriously soothing for
your kind as the ones you call spiritual
—that's it, you somehow understand
that the way your hand stirs that
cooking food is not just a matter of
kitchen expertise but a perfect
opportunity to increase the power
that being human represents, a power
most humans believe is heaven-sent,
they don't comprehend what you so
obviously do, that the difference
between us and you is not that you
have to do so many lowly things to
get through just a few hours, but
that if you do these things with
love, then that exceeds all the powers
any gods could possess, and you are
nothing less than the object of a
god's desire, not to make you a
goddess, but to be made human by the
caress of your hand as you take his
arm to get warm in the night chill
he can finally feel through you—
no wonder the gods and goddesses

keep telling themselves they have
it so much better than you, if they
for one moment could experience the
feeling of pure love you seem to
put into everything you do, there
wouldn't be any gods or goddesses
left up there to talk to, they'd
all be down here competing with me
for the chance to see you open a
door, pick your glove up off the
floor, give a little girl more of
what she's asking for, your love—
even the little girl I see inside
of you, who doesn't need me to
take care of her because you've
done that so well—hell, what's
a god to do with a human like you
who doesn't need any of my godlike
tricks and omnipotence? how I long
for the common sense of an ordinary
man who understands just when and
how to take your hand in his—
oh yes, a god can be awestruck too,
once he has seen you—

On the other hand, and maybe more
realistically, you make me feel
like I am the mortal man, struggling
to get by all these years, and getting
by, sometimes only by getting high,
but not anymore, and then suddenly
there you are, a goddess come down

from on high, to grace me with
your presence for reasons I can't
guess but worry I'll mess up in
my clumsiness as I try to let you
know that I will go as slow as you
will let me in getting to know you
because I want this revelation to
last forever, this uncovering of
your goddess essence which makes
the most humble tasks look like
gestures of a love so profound—as
Selby says, wherever we seek God
we meet him, and that is holy ground,
so everywhere you are is holy and
God is found, and okay, it isn't
that you're a goddess and I'm just
a man that makes me forget all
my little schemes and plans that
worked with the other girls, it's
that the way you carry your human
qualities, that dignity and grace
with which you move from place to
place to place and chore to chore
is more than any god could aspire
to, and so in you, I see the truth
that this is truly the dwelling
place of the gods—of the one
God—and every human is a god and
goddess too, and it is you I owe
for allowing me to feel that I am
too, that my age is perfect and
so is my height, that it's okay to
look nice and even be white, that
I too can take my place among the

human gods and goddesses without
fear or judgement or false pride,
that I too can be the man I truly
am and yet still take care of and
share the little boy inside, that
anywhere we humans reside—but
I have to admit for me, especially
anywhere you might be—is truly
paradise.

IN THE MOOD

I'm too tired to talk, or write, or . . .
It's been three days now together and
I'm afraid to feel so comfortable with
someone I didn't even know two weeks ago,
it's like coming home to the home I only
imagined but never knew, it's like
meeting myself in a woman who has been
where I've been and made it through too,
it's like staying up all night talking
and kissing and sucking and fucking or
trying to, getting self-conscious and
afraid that this could be it—could it?—
not perfection or gods and goddesses,
but a friend, a cohort, a partner, a
fox who won't quit even if my dick does.
That doesn't sound like the kind of
thing I want to read to a roomful of
people, but she wouldn't care if I did,
her light and mine, no matter what color
or how powerful the flame, no longer have
to be hid, if they ever were, because
like me there's a fire in her that has
been fueled by years of facing the truth,
of disarming shame, yet keeping her
innocence and playfulness and hope,
the qualities we usually confuse with youth,
even though the young are so old in so many
ways, killing themselves over fears and
frustrations that now only rarely disturb
our days—hey, I don't want to be the daddy
anymore, and with her I don't have to be,

well, maybe now and then in bed but only for
a change from all the ways we can imagine
of being together, and I don't need tears to
turn me on, or to be desperately needed to come,
or fears that she will run when she sees
I'm only a man and not the sun, I don't
even need someone who needs to be won anymore,
I have all I need in my life without her,
but what I want, what I'm in the mood for
is a woman more my size, a match, an equal,
one I can't pin down unless she wants me to,
who can sit across a table the first time we
have breakfast in, and even out, and read
the paper, and when she starts to speak it isn't
a shout about how I'm ignoring her but a
quote from an article she's reading that
ends up starting a discussion just between
us that makes the paper nothing more than
it is, yesterday's news, abridged, remote,
and nowhere near as interesting as her, as us,
a woman I can talk to another woman around
and not expect a frown of insecurity and
disapproval and neglect to be my punishment
because she trusts that what we have between
us is real enough to incorporate the rest
of our lives and the people in them, a woman
who talks to me from her heart and her experience
and her common sense and not some latest
best-seller about the emotional expense of
being a woman who loves too much or loving
men who can't pay the rent or live up to
all the potential the author saw in some man
whose failures or rejections are now historical
events, a woman who can hold me in her arms

for hours just because it's comfortable that
way today and not because she needs to feel
a neediness in me that I don't have but she
needs, to feel needed, and all that stuff that
women who like to act tough usually feed on—
no way—I'm in the mood for a woman who can
get the kind of looks from men that made me want
to mutilate them once, way back when I was
always insecure behind the cool that attracted
women that got those looks from men like
I was pretending to be, but now I want to
see them stare and not have to glare any
threatening looks their way but just feel
good that no matter how hard they look,
or what enticing words they say, she ain't
going away from what we have, because I
haven't given her any reasons to—yeah,
I want a woman who will know that the
most important words don't have to be said,
that it's in what you do, not what's in your
head, and then she does them and makes me
want to do those things too, and then I do—
in other words beautiful, I want a woman
just like you.

OBSESSION, POSSESSION, AND DOING TIME

Of course I want to possess
whatever I'm obsessed with—
that Bonnard painting in the Phillips Gallery in Washington DC
that I visited at least three times a week
for the years I lived a few blocks away
until one day they moved it—so I moved
back to New York where I was obsessed with the same old stuff
like poetry, and city rain,
the corners of certain
city blocks and buildings,
the way the traffic lights glowed so bright against the sky
as day begins to turn to night—
the drugs that made me think
I needed them to see that—
the dreams of making my mark on the world
in ways that would make up
for all the times the world
tripped me up, threw another
obstacle in my path, smacked
me down, kicked me around,
beat and battered me into
an arrogance so powerful
people thought it was really
me, so did I for a while,
and with a style always so out front and unique,
or so I wanted to believe,
other poets and artists would
seek me out to discover what
they were doing next—like

moving to L.A. where the look
of neon at that magic time of
day when the sun goes down
became a new obsession that I
found I didn't need the old
drugs to dig or enjoy or even
comprehend—I got to lend my obsessions out again
until I saw them on the screen
and heard them on the radio—
and I thought this is a funny
way to go—I'm out here learning
how to grow beyond the petty
drives that drove me into self-
obsessive possessiveness with
all that mattered to the point
of being shattered into billions
of bits of the memories I thought made up my life—
and then I thought there is
no way to mend myself, I need
some help—and I got it—
I'm still the same obsessive fighter
for the dreams I'll never give up
whether you still see them in my eyes
or not—I got to possess what I'm
obsessed with just as much as ever,
to the point I want to be it—I
wanted to be that painting by Bonnard,
or the rain, or the glowing traffic light
or neon bright against the darkening blue—
or you—and I was and am—I always knew that—yes,
I am the obsession, and I am the possession,
and I am the time that's being done—
and that's just life as I unfold it
day by day and not some universal

contest to be lost or won—I'm
grateful every night for the bed I sleep in
and every morning for the sun or clouds or rain—
which doesn't mean I'm not ambitious
or that being with you is not the most
delicious way of spending whatever time is mine—
hey, I'm grateful for all my dreams and visions—
especially the one called you—
but I also love the way I'm
letting go of having to possess
all that I'm obsessed with and
letting time do me for a change—
speaking of change, I'd like to be possessed for a while
and be the object of somebody
else's style not just this
not-so-neutral-Jersey-cowboy-hipster-
nice-guy-but-don't-get-too-close-cool-
master-of-my-universe in which I'm
always generous and never act out of spite—
I know that ain't quite the way you see it,
so straighten me out, get a ruler
and draw new lines, make me climb
your mountains and ford your streams
until your dreams are mine and I'm
in them with you, especially
the ones that come true, which
they all do if we let them—
we just might not be there to get them when they do—
so com'ere let's drop a tear
and swap a kiss and reminisce
about the way we want it to be,
until we can see it so clearly
nothing can keep us from getting there—
even when we already are—

you know the dream—it's
the one where we're finally truly understood—
understand?

THAT FEELING WHEN IT FIRST GOES IN

"I am the poet of sin" said Whitman,
or something like that in my head.
I want you in my bed right now more
than I want all the junk in all the
stores you can't resist. You kept on
insisting that you needed to be alone.
Like Garbo supposedly never said.
I have been alone in this bed since
the last time you were here. I remember
the first woman to call me "dear" just
like in the movies. I wasn't sure I
liked it. The few girls who did that
back when the movies really were the
movies, sounded too American or maybe
Protestant or something foreign from
the Irish-American women I grew up around.
Or even the few blacks. None of them
called their men "dear." That was
something from *Father Knows Best,*
back when television was really tele-
vision. What an idea, to tell a
vision, sort of another description
of poetry. Yo, check it out, here I
am again at the typewriter speeding
two-fingered around these keys, trying
to locate the place where the motion
toward life originates in me, not you,
because we're through, at least until
we get to that time when we can be

friends, as if I didn't already have
enough beautiful women friends in my
life who once were lovers until they
discovered I'm not the man of their
dreams, I'm just an old guy in jeans
who talks like a kid because he never
did get it that all everybody wants is
a man to decide what should be done
and then to go ahead and do it—
not sit around and write poems about
how empty the bed is without you—No shit.

I OVERWHELMED HER WITH MY NEED

I couldn't help it.
This feeling in my chest
of more than emptiness,
like a vacuum sucking my spirit, my soul,
my personality, my character,
my life away . . . without her.
I placed my life and my will in her hands,
turned them over to her care.
The same mistake I always make,
because the rush is always so incredibly
satisfying when that first fluttery
female response at being dug so deeply
is expressed . . . but then, then,
it looks like pressure, like being
crowded, like maybe you ain't mister
perfect mister right mister fairhaired boy
mister cool mister strong and handsome and
the answer to her prayers after all.
You might just be mister weak sometimes,
mister needy, mister let me love you
every heartbeat for the rest of your life.
And they choke on that, they lose their
breath for the first time in a scary way,
not that orgasmic exciting ecstasy way,
and they don't want it,
they want to push it away
so they can breathe, because
they don't need you that bad,
they can't afford to: this is the new world
and they are the new girls
and they got some better things to do

real soon with maybe better people
and you're less-than again,
you're not-good-enough again,
you're the sprinter who passes everybody else
for the first few days and then
can't keep up, get weak and wobbly
and need somebody to lean on,
only love ain't about leaning yet,
it's got to be going on for a while,
or maybe it just can't be that way anymore,
it's too much to ask in the modern world,
we're talking financial insecurity
and career moves and confidence and
courses in ways to become the best you
you've ever been even if that means
leaving some people behind,
you've done it too, all your life,
maybe it's karma, maybe it's nostalgia,
maybe it's what goes around comes around
as you watch the guys on top
pursue her too and all you can do
is float away on the flood
of your own self-pity and lack of control
'cause those feelings in your heart
are part of what makes you honest,
only they don't want honest
they want righteous they want better-than
they want stand up and be a man and
get your emotional insecurities under control
and out of sight for the duration,
'cause this is war boy
and we got a lot more battles to fight
and if you're gonna lay down and whine
and ask for mercy and stroking and

semi-adoration like you got from those
lesser girls, you're in the wrong outfit,
you belong behind the lines
not out front here where they make heroes
out of guys who don't succumb
to the fear and fatigue and frustration
and false interpretations
of a reality nobody will ever really know
let alone understand anyway . . .
Know what I mean?

I'M AFRAID I'M GONNA START

crying & never stop—

I'm afraid I'll never cry—

FOOLS FOR LOVE

and light and music
fools for God and essences of lives
fools for
food and sex and highs inexplicable
fools for lavender and shades of gray and
billions of whatever can be counted that way
fools for missions improbable, ventures into
the unknown of each other's wills
fools for gladiolas and roses and ferns that grow
like weeds and are weeds for all we know
that can be said to be
the fools we see when we begin to see
as only bargain hunters do
when on a spree in some far-off commercial market
for the wares we spared our hearts when what we wanted
was to be the fools of a love
so grandiose that most people would die before embracing—
but we aren't most, we are the rest
that were left to be the fools I grew up loving
when I thought of Saint Francis and his love
of poverty and every living creature and was known
for such overtures to nature that
no one understood but were impressed with anyway
even me—even when I dropped away
from all things Catholic I had grown up with
he still figured as my mentor in some unarticulated way—
"God's Fool" they called him, as I wouldn't mind being called
today, because I see this God as the spirit of the universe,
and how much I'd rather be a fool for that force than
for the ones that force me to stoop to places not beneath me
but beneath the floor of discards that has been our undoing,

I mean the fool in the Tarot deck was who I always identified
with and the court fools and tribal fools who were always
granted the liberty to point out the foibles of emperors and
chiefs whose clothes were nonapparent like those at
the Oscars last night where I took so much delight in
Satyajit Ray's acceptance from a hospital bed in Calcutta
and his getting back at Ginger Rogers for not answering his
fan letter when he was young and still impressed with
Hollywood the way we all are when we're young and I
never don't want to be, not with the schemes and cynicism of
the bankers and their pimps but with the dreams and humanism
of the fools for love who would use the magic of the tribal
screen to imagine for us who we might be or become
even those of us who have no time to be because we are
so lost in others, even us fools for love which is just
another way of saying poets to my mind and heart and
way of starting over in the poem that has always been my
safest haven where a home can always be found for the
fools for love we might all be if we were left alone to be
whoever we were before they got ahold of us—
enough, I'm crazy from trying and trying is only buying time,
eventually we have to do or not do and tonight
I want to do it all again, again

yeah, it's true, I interrupt you
when you're talking and dream of being in a
presidential debate, and when I talk you think I'm dying
to impress with all the little facts and anecdotes I've
gleaned from all the years of inability to resist the
printed matter of my life—I'm quiet sometimes too and
then you think I may be ignoring you for some inner
distraction, and that's probably true too, I'm a
writer and a dreamer and I like to think about
everything all the time

but in no way does that diminish the love I feel for you
and all the yous I end up ignoring—
hey, I'm pouring my heart out here, don't
dismiss it so quickly, it is possible to love
and seem aloof at the same time, I'm living proof
of that, not that I don't get down to where the ground
meets our more profound sexual ambitions either teaser,
I'm here, not there, and all the air we share in
this tight room is empty of the doom you project
when you don't think any of it might last or
ultimately matter, except as fodder for the
ammunition you will use in coming affairs with
men whose airs are not the kind we breath but
suffocate under—at least when I blunder through
your defenses and finally make contact, the struggle
that ensues is only with the bodily logistics of
who's pursued and who pursues, like in the movie
Basic Instinct but without the violence . . .
and Michael Douglas.

LOST ANGELS 2

The angel of fear and the angel
of self-consciousness, the
angel of never enough and the
angel of too fucking much,
the angel of nicotine and the
angel of caffeine, the angel of
New Jersey and the angel of
Colorado, the angel of nakedness
and the angel of covering up,
the angel of discontent and
the angel of serendipity, the
angel of loose and appropriately
sexy female energy and the angel
of overly flirtatious and
inappropriately seductive male
attention, the angel of too many
jokes and the angel of repressed
resentment, the angel of feeling
safe in the relationship enough
to make you think she might
leave it for you and the angel
of talent gone unrecognized,
the angel of no talent and
the angel of knowing how to
make money on that, the angel
of the unrelenting love jones
and the angel of music too
loud and acoustics too stupid
to hear someone sitting at
the same table, the angel of
being alone in the same old

crowd of other lonely people
and the angel of wanting to
be naked and turned on by
too many unavailable people,
the angel of not enough sleep
and the angel of too much
competitiveness, the angel
of unappreciation and the
angel of pride, the angel
of lost causes and the angel
of perfectionism, the angel
of communism and the angel of
children of '60s communes,
the angel of deceptive quietness
and the angel of deceptive good
looks, the angel of you can't
judge a book by its cover and
the angel of too many books,
the angel of rap and the angel
of funk, the angel of Aaron
Copland and the angel of Elvis
Aron Presley, the angel of
business enthusiasts and the
angel of Harley self-righteousness,
the angel of civilians and the
angel of the too hip, the angel
of geography and the angel of
pollution, the angel of lesbians
who like to be sexually dominated
now and then by politically
correct men and the angel of
gay male jocks, the angel of
unproduced scripts and the angel
of unknown history, the angel

of once where we all had been
and the angel of never getting
there, the angel of honoring
one's path and the angel of
divine dissatisfaction, the
angel of you and the angel
of me and the angel we run from
when the angel we become is
the unacknowledged star of
our universe and our universe
is changing too fast to grasp
with so little as the love we
forgot we had for all the
lost angels that watch over
us even when we don't believe—

LAST NIGHT

I got into a lot of fights
when I was growing up—
a couple a week until I was 22—
then I got married
to a girl I hardly knew—
it seemed at the time
like the right thing to do—
but until then I was so afraid
that you all thought I was afraid
that it filled me with a rage
so deep and blue nobody ever knew
who I was going to throw through
the nearest window—me or you—
a lot of broken glass in my past—
a lot of broken past in my glass
back then too—some of it wasn't
even true—like when I'd tell some
stranger all about you, and we hadn't
even met—in fact, we haven't
yet—even though last night I felt
my tongue slip through your lips again
until it found your tongue and the doors
of the universe shut behind them leaving
them all alone to do their tongue dance
and my brainwaves got lost in all that
sensuous darkness while somewhere outside
it I could smell your hair and feel your
solid softness filling my arms until we
were so close I could see out the back
of you and into the eyes of some buddies
I grabbed your behind to impress, even

though I already knew there wasn't anything
more than kissing that we were gonna do
because that's all I wanted to—and it was
enough, like back in the '50s when I tried
so hard to be tough, even in my dreams where
I was always the star of all the teams and
won all the games for you—now the games
don't mean so much to me, but you still
do—only I always wake up wondering, who
the fuck are you?

ATTITUDE AND BEATITUDE

ah, it's a melancholy,
melancholy, melancholy
race I come from—
with "Sacred Hearts" all
suffering hanging over
our childhood beds and
even the redheads in our
past—Grandma Rose
McBride from Galway—
or the red blood streaming
from my finger today when
I cut the flowers sent for
my birthday from a man
I hardly know & not
the woman I—my kids
are grown—I'm home
alone on my 48th birth-
day watching—what?—
not you—you're dead
and all that's left are
these pictures of the people
you knew who I never
cared about—and the
kids who I did—and
me and you—that
blonde keeps getting a
little loaded and telling
me I'm white as if
I didn't know that—I
knew that long ago—
I'm so white the skin

on my stomach gives
off the glow of newly
fallen snow—as if I
might be cold or no
longer alive—but I
am—you aren't—or
all these things from
some earlier version
of my life—or someone
else's—oh tonight,
tonight, I wanted to
be alone—and I—
you can't even phone—
remember how we did?
there was a home there
once—I called it you
& you were so in love
with the gentle side
of what I remember
as rage—huh—that
page has crumbled—
it fell apart in my
hands—little spots of
red from where I cut
off the tip of my
finger with the
scissors I use to trim
the rosebush in
front of this house
where I live like a
widow on a small
pension that's running
out—and her?—I
haven't seen her since

before you—but
she's alive I'm sure—
back home in Costa
Rica with—I miss
her too—I miss you—
differently—and how can
they ever know what we
knew—or how many
dead there are inside my
heart & head to fill
this bed I still laugh
when I come in—and
the women sometimes
find that strange—or
scary—thank God some
find it nice or sexy or—
no—who cares—I laugh
to find out once again
I'm still alive!—me—
of all of us—I made
it all this way—my
forty-fucking-eighth
birthday—the lady
I laughed with last is
half my age and likes
it—why?—because I
don't demand too much—
because I have that
slow and gentle touch
I learned with you—oh
oh oh—sometimes
it's too slow—with all
the memories crowding
in between breaths—

God, help me make it
through the days—
the nights are easy—
I can be whoever
I am then—when
the lights go out and
so do I—stay up
tonight and keep my
spirit company—
alone again on purpose
but without delight—
I want my due, God,
from this world of
people I have nurtured
and inspired—I want
them to understand
how tired I am and
forgive me if I sometimes
seem distracted or
forgetful or pissed off—
it's only because I'm
thinking of you and
you and all the yous
I knew so intimately
who have passed—all
thinking they'd be
around long after me—
but see, I had to raise
my kids—and now I
want to watch them
go out into the world
and find out who they
are and maybe have
their own—so let me

stick around until my
kids' kids are all grown—
if that's possible to do—
and let me be the eyes
and ears and consciousness
of you, who went
before me & never knew
how life might have
turned out—this is how—

TURNING 50

It's like turning 21
only in reverse
—a milestone
not a millstone,
it could be worse,
I remember my
21st—my friends
gave me a big party—
I was the only white
guy there—by
the time they got
the cake together we
were all so wasted
we couldn't find the
candles, or light them,
or blow them out—
one of the guys
started to
cry & when our
hostess asked him why
he said because he was
sure I wouldn't see 22
the way I lived back then—
well, I guess I showed them

even if I am a little tired today—
it's not because I'm turning 50 okay?—
or because I celebrated yesterday,
or stayed up too late and got up too early
for the past few days, or because I
got a tattoo that's older than you
and that kind of stuff seems to matter

to the few who don't know yet that the
differences are there for enticement
and celebration, not to justify some
fear of the unknown—it's all knowable—
and I know I've said it before and it
seems kind of corny, even when I blame
it on Selby, but like he says, it's
all love and either we let fear get
in the way of that or not—*not* is
what I vote for—what I'm tired of
is the way that fear goes around from
one sad clown to another, beating each
other down for what somebody else did
to them—the sin we saw on that
video—which one depends on where
you're viewing it from, they say—but
I don't say that—I say somebody beats
up on that defenseless guy because
somebody else beat up on them once—
sounds too simple doesn't it?—I
know, it's more complex than that,
but I really don't care today—I've
watched a lot of people live and die
in my time, and most have been beaten
by someone or something at some time or
another and some let it kill them and
some used it as an excuse to kill
somebody else and some never got over
it and some of us got over it again
and again, but when your number's called
it don't matter where you been it
matters where you are, and I want to
be right smack in the middle of love,
the kind that comes from above and
makes everything possible . . .

3 POSTSCRIPT
(WHERE DO WE BELONG?)

WHERE DO WE BELONG

for Neal Peters, Terence Winch, and John McCarthy

Passing through these hills, these lakes,
these fates I thought I had outwitted—
who am I here? in the land of my
fathers—this harsh wind & chill, the
sheets of rain lashing out like my
anger at meager perspectives on life
despite all the vistas the world has
forgotten—I am *myself*—the *himself*
of this life I'm given—& when the
rain clears—or goes soft—the land-
scapes pull my heart to peaks of
awe & wonder—how could this be?
so much beauty must be graced with
the living lace of showers, the veils
of a reality too God-like to endure—
ah—I'm happy—& confused—like a
lover returning after rejection & recon-
ciliation—what do I expect to find?
the answer to my dreams.

An uncle long dead—the "gentle"
one his wife compared me to—
his nose, his chin, his manly smile—
in this cousin "once removed" it
took me days to find—he once
lived in the same thatched
cottage my grandfather rose every
morning in, from the day he was
born until he left for distant
shores—& us—the family he would

have—the kids, in fear & arrogance,
rejecting what he was in all their
American striving—after what?
what we have now & find so
lacking in fulfillment we have to
slam & shoot & burn the mother-
fucker down before it's ours?—
it took me 50 years to find that
thatched-roof cottage, uninhabited
for only four, still standing, not for
many more—& maybe me too.

Or him—this cousin Paddy—
69—a bachelor—the last of
"our Lallys" in County Galway where
I first went to see the famous bay
& was disappointed & excited all at
once—it was an August day but the
dampness & chill in the air made it
necessary for me to wear a coat, which
wasn't even enough when the wind
began to blow—dark clouds filled the sky—
rain fell sporadically—the water could
not have looked less inviting—darker
than any I've ever seen outside of dreams—
& choppy, like a major winter storm
was brewing, when everywhere else I
had just been—L.A., New York—my friends
& family were stewing in the end-of-summer
heat waves of our new world order
weather—but here, in Galway, sweaters
were the order of the day—& no way
would anybody be able to see through the
thick sky cover any moon going
down on any bay—

                      & I had all I
could do to keep on my side of the
"highway," which meant any road big
enough for two cars to pass without
a heart attack, as I tried to get
away from the toylike streets of
Galway City, so narrow they were best
suited for donkey carts and the
proverbial wheelbarrow, not compact
cars like the one I'm having trouble
negotiating through this *faux* rush
hour when I accidentally bump a car
in front of me and out jumps a young
lady yelling things like "stupid" at
me & all I can do is roll down my
window & explain I'm not used to
driving on this side of the road
or car because I'm from America—
"Well, I'm not!" she shouts as she
shakes her head at I guess what
must be a rare occurrence, although
I can't see why since they all drive,
as McCarthy says, like Indians who
just got ahold of their first ponies.

& where are they all off to anyway
on an island not big enough to take
that long to reach the edges of—
nowhere, I discover, as they pass
me going 85 & I'm just trying not
to slide off into the hedges or
the stone walls that line these
country roads, because when I
come around the next bend, there

they are, backed up and waiting
patiently while someone drives
their cows on home, or stops to
chat up a neighbor—no honking
horns, no impatient scorn, no
guns drawn, just acceptance of
the situation—until it's time
to move again—& then they're
off, around blind curves with
little enough room for two cars
going opposite directions, let
alone a third trying to make
a move straight down the middle
at 85 or 90, & me still trying
to remember which side is mine.

& then there they are—the
"fields of Athenry" celebrated
in song and family legend—I
know my grandfather came from
nearby & wonder if these stone
walls and almost treeless views
were ones he knew, the rich
green meadows & pastures, the
sheep & cows & occasional bandy-
legged dog looking out on it all
as if it could care less about
the rest of the world, including
me passing by on my way to three
days of leads to "Lallys" who
are no relations—much gossip
of who married whom & church records,
only the wrong church, sending
me to suspicious farmers who

ignore the hand I extend until
they come to understand I don't
want anything more than the
lore of my family.

I get led on by one who comes off
like Richard Harris in *The Field*
the movie the folks I'm staying
with say is the one about their
country they found most real—
& so did I—that angry patriarch
so narrow-minded & mean & yet
somehow heroic, reminding me
of my grandfather & what I
remembered of a man who always
seemed to scowl & need a shave
& dress like a bum & have been
drinking, that stinking smell
of alcohol & old worn-for-years-
through-everything-that-mattered
clothes, still sturdy though,
like him the neighbors saw as the
local character, but to us he was
"Himself," the father of our clan.

And now here I am where he began,
following one false lead after another,
meeting available widows ten years
my senior, whose brothers point out
ruins of peasant huts they swear
is where my grandfather grew up,
the stones so tightly fitted, like
the walls all around this country,
"knitted" as they say, so that

even without mortar or cement they
can withstand water or contain
bulls, except the human ones—
the interlocking shapes & sizes
keeping out the wind & rain while
the thatched roofs equally as
intricate keep the water out too
& the warmth in—these places
fascinate me, each one could be
a place my grandfather knew.

I don't mind the dead ends
because they all lead to the
kitchens of farmhouses where
everyone seems ready to share
a bottle or some tea and an
anecdote about the ones now
gone across the sea, some never
known or long forgotten, their
children or grandchildren turning
up "back home" so many years later,
like me, here now, trying to uncover
what? the answer to my never being
able to identify with who I was
brought up with & wondering why—

But now I'm sharing some bread or
sandwiches or cakes when they
take me to the oldest living
memory in the neighborhood to ask
"Do you remember any Lallys
in these parts, ones who
went away?" & I say "In the
last century, late 1800s, he

died in 1956" and they reply
"That's not so long ago, someone
should know if he came back for
visits, as you say, now that'd
be something to remember then,
a Yank coming home in the '30s
or '40s would be an event, sure
it would"—& I could almost feel
myself relaxing, something old
& familiar in these scenes, not
just the fear I had of my Irish
grandparents but the closeness—
they were always there, right
down the street, waiting for me
to come & greet them as my mother
always made me do at least once a
week—I only wish I knew then what
I know so I could have slowed
down those brief encounters &
maybe remember—what?—what
I think I'm feeling now—the
comfort & ease of being at peace
with who you are—I am.

When, through some unacknowledged
or too subtle for my eyes and ears
decision is reached and it's
time to go, no one remembering
my grandfather "Mike," someone
suggesting another little place with its
own name, despite the fact that it isn't
on the map & all it means is a handful
of houses more or less close
by each other, and another

peat fire in the kitchen heating
stove, and the best chair, closest
to the heat, to be my place,
and there's no haste at all
to get on with their farmer's day,
& I get the impression these
people would rather talk than
work anyway, & they'd rather
hear a poem recited than talk
& why recite a poem if someone
can sing a song all the way through—
they just know what they like best,
& it seems to be the articulation
of the human mind at rest & glad of it.

Finally I get in touch with "my
brother the priest" as we say,
who has lived in Japan these 30
years or more & who had once
come looking around here maybe
that long ago—he tells me
the place to look is called Bookeen,
another handful of houses where some
relatives lived but with a different
last name, having descended from one
of Grandpa's sisters who stayed
behind, but there is no use,
he says, looking Grandpa up in
the local church because our
Lallys had gone somewhere else,
the "Redemptorist monastery"
a few miles the other way—
& when I tell this to the man of the
house where I am staying, he says

"I know your man, I'm sure he's
related for his name is Lally &
he lives at Tallyho Cross" (which
I later learn means crossroads)
"not far from Bookeen but closer to
Esker"—the Redemptorist place—

& he takes me to see this Paddy
Lally in an old "two-story" as
they call them when they are,
"too dilapidated" to invite me
in, he tells my host, so he comes
out to the car instead and gets
in the back and we shake hands
and I see something familiar in
the strength of his nose and
unshaven chin and the look in
his eye and even the way his old
clothes are worn & thick with
accumulated what can I call it
but life? it's hard to describe
without sounding the way "the
Americans" did when they talked of
my grandfather, only worse,
like a homeless person might
look now, not even that good
in a way, what can I say? he
wears a suit coat that has seen
better days a long long time ago—
obviously he works in it,
lives in it, maybe every day—
but he has a full head of hair
and as much on his upper cheeks
as if he had forgotten to shave

there—later I will discover
in a book that it was traditional
for the Irish men of the West to
let their face hair grow and only
shave it for special occasions
but never the hair in their nose
or low on their throat or upper
cheeks, a sign of their connection
to the past, their fathers and
theirs, but now he only looks
like he had missed the hairs
a long time ago—

          Anyway, I
say my grandfather's name was
Michael, like mine, & my father's
name was James—he says his
father's name was Frank & I say
I had an uncle Frank, & he says
his grandfather's name was Pat
& I say my great-grandfather's name
was that, and the other man points
out that my grandfather came back
for visits & wouldn't he remember
that and Paddy says "Ah, it was a
long time ago" and looks me in
the eye and with a sort of sigh
says "There was a priest here
once from America, he lived in
Japan, but I never met him"—
"That'd be my brother" I say—
"You know, you can go over to
Galway City and find a book on names
that'll tell you all you'd want to

know about the Lallys, not us though,
but about the name—ah, but
what's in a name" he goes on "a
rose by any other name would
smell as sweet, wasn't it Mister
Shakespeare said that—" he doesn't
really ask, a kind of glow in
his eye as though he's trying to
put one by me as I smile & reply
"That's so, Shakespeare said that,
and maybe you're right, I'm content
to just be here, near where I know
my grandfather came from—it's enough."

& then he looks at me again, as if
seeing something else & says real low,
as though throwing it away, "I remember
Mike" & the hairs on the back of
my neck stand up—"He used to take
Patsy Lally into Athenry to the pubs,
Patsy liked his drink, Mike was
alright . . . " and I am home again in
my heart, this is the start of
something bigger than I remembered
or expected, because it is so simple
& so everyday, as we sit there in
my host's little car, Paddy in the back,
the two of them sharing a smoke, Paddy
quiet again, and looking at his big,
gnarly hands and not at us, as my host
begins to figure out the dates & how
it is we are or might be related,
Paddy & me, ". . . aye, then Paddy's
father is your grandfather's youngest

brother, which would make Paddy here
you father's first cousin & your
first cousin once removed . . ."

We all mull over that, me looking out
at the incredible display of clouds
that jam up the Irish sky in ever
more complicated ways, creating that
just-before-a-storm-begins deep silvery
light I always loved when I was a kid
& still do & would always stop
whatever I was doing to sit and stare
as I'm doing now, this is me, doing
what I always loved to do, attracted
to this view as if I knew it & these
two men who seem to know it, & therefore,
maybe me, too—& finally our host says,
"You know, Michael lives out
in California near Hollywood
& works sometimes in the fill-im business"
& without missing a beat Paddy says "I
hear that business isn't doing so good
these days" & then goes on to say "Maybe
you'd remember who said, after shaking
hands on a deal, 'This contract isn't
worth the paper it's written on'" &
I smile & say "Sam Goldwyn," having read
maybe the same source he had,
& Paddy nods into his gnarled & cupped
hands & the cigarette smoke they
seem to embrace "Aye, that'd be Mister
Goldwyn said that—would you like to
see where your grandfather lived?"

The place is called "Tallyho Cross"
because it's where they once kept
the kennels for the hunting dogs
back when the landlords ruled
this land & my grandfather's clan
lived in the thatched-roof cottage
Paddy grew up in & takes us to now—
someone else lived there until four
years ago, and now it's on its way
to slow decay or what they call being
"knocked," for "knocked down," I guess,
like all the ruins that dot this
countryside, they don't mean knocked
down by human hands, that would be
"tumbled," an older term from harsher
times when that's what the landlord
and British would do to those whose
meager potato crops might fail &
the law of the land would prevail,
being he who owns it gets to eat &
he who doesn't gets to starve or
somehow get away to foreign lands—

But on this day I have returned from
one and as I stand before this ancient
peasant place where my grandfather
first faced the life he would live,
I remember a song my father would
sing as he shaved & gave himself his
morning "Jewish bath," meaning splashing
water on himself from the stopped-up
tiny bathroom sink while we all waited
our turn, dreading the puddles we would
find but kind of digging the lines of

the music lilting our way from behind the
bathroom door, which were more or less:
"Oh my name is" I always thought he next
sang "Paddy Lee" but maybe it was "Pat
Lally" and went on "I'm an Irishman you
see, I was born in County Galway, Tallyho—"

I always thought that last was some
sort of exclamation, not a place, but
here it is, the ancestral home, not
even a bone's throw from where the kennels
once stood & now I stand, & Paddy
explains how the old thatch roof cottage
won't last much longer because when
the fire goes out—a flame that
may have burned unrelentingly for
centuries, can you imagine?—
the moisture seeps in and begins to
make the place uninhabitable &
slowly it begins to rot and then
cave in, but not before I made it
here to see it & to stand before it
on the dark green grass fed by these
manic clouds and it all feels so
familiar in ways I would have dismissed
if you'd told me all this just days
before—& then there was more.

More time just being ourselves, alone,
together there, in that damp crisp
brilliantly pure of pollution air,
until Paddy says "Would you like to
see the house where John Huston
lived?" & of course I say sure—

it's nearby, one of the old "big
houses" that once was the landlords—
an Englishman lives there now but
that doesn't stop my host from driving
up the long driveway as if it was
his own, or parking right before the
front door so we can get a good long
look—& Paddy tells a story of
the way it was in the days of the
landlords, when my grandfather was a
boy, when two boys, much like he
must have been, decide to ambush the
landlord on his way home, so they
wait by the road for him to pass
as he does every day, only two hours
after he should have come the one
turns to the other & says "I hope
the poor man hasn't had an accident"
—& the humor in that, if you can't
see it, is that he meant it, & so
did his friend, as Paddy said "That's
the way they were then" & sometimes
still are, because they would shoot
the man just the same—oh what's in
a name—

For the next few days Paddy takes me
around to meet others who might remember
my grandfather or more lore about the family
than he seems to care about but thinks I do—
like the 92-year-old woman whose memory
would be the longest in that small
place—her name is Rose like my
grandmother's & she has a face that

glows with health & interest & a
sparkle in her eye that makes me think
she's being flirtatious—she's in
fine shape, as most of them seem to be,
despite the fatty ham they call bacon
& rashers & tons of bread & jam & quarts
of strong tea—in fact, she moves &
speaks & remembers local history like
the women back in L.A. who work out &
run & meditate half the day & are only
20- or 30-something—she lives alone
across the road from her daughter &
that daughter's school-aged farmer sons
& schoolteacher daughter & another one
who is a "scholar" too, as they call
all students here—they all seem
caught up in the details of their
history & more, the international farm &
political scene & their place in all that—

I'm surprised & delighted at how well-
read they all seem to be, especially
Paddy, who is quiet—& much like a
man who lives alone—in the kitchens
of these homes he takes me to where
he is nonetheless treated with great
respect—as a "good man," a "decent
man," who never did anyone harm but
sometimes did them good—& it seems
to be understood that dress &
appearance mean nothing in this
neighborhood—although the kids
look hip enough when they get
dressed up to go dancing around ten—

that seems to be the style—
stay up late if you can & have a
good time & nobody will mind because
what else is life for but to sing
& dance & drink & eat & talk like
you didn't care where the next dollar
or pound is coming from, even if some
of the talk would make you think
they do—although my host, a man
my age but with four kids still at
home, the one where I'm staying, says
"Ah, the rich don't seem happy though,
now do they Michael?" & what can I say,
never really having been that way—
rich—myself, &—happy? I'm not
sure I even know what it means, though
it seems to be coming clearer as I sit
among these people maybe I can call my
own—

I could have stayed all night
in every country kitchen
Paddy took me to—or sat in the
car or waited out the rain in a
cow shed while he smoked & we
both lived in our heads & if I
spoke he would always reply with
a quote, not in any arrogant
showoff way, but kind of shy,
as if to say, now what about
this, doesn't this apply? that
somebody else said—& it always
did—the man quoted Buddha
& Montezuma to me when I mentioned

stuff that had to do with peace
or Mexico—how did he know?—
this man who lived alone in the
middle of nowhere with no car,
just an old well-used bike, the few
neighborhood boys helping him out
by mowing the land around his
house so he could get in and out
to the road—& him helping
others with this & that down in
the fields & the bogs in his old
dark-stained suit coat & unshaven
face & big gnarly hands & manly
smile—I fell in love with his
way & his manner & the fact that
he obviously was as addicted as I
am to words on the page as they
express worlds in the minds & the
lives of others so far from us—

I never knew—my father with his
seventh-grade education tried so hard
to be American he withdrew from
all that had to do with books,
except the Catholic ones, & I
somehow got the impression the people
I came from were illiterate & I
was the anomaly & would feel
fucked up for wanting to read &
write poetry & be who I am instead
of what my father thought America
wanted him to be—but now I know,
Paddy told me, that his grandfather,
my grandfather's father Pat, loved

to read, & had a special fondness
for history, as so many here do,
not knowing who the latest "star"
in the USA might be, or caring,
but remembering some long gone
ancestral feat of only local renown
or the deeper nuances & subtleties of
the European story that never quite
reached this far, the very edge of
that world, facing the Atlantic that
I stick my hands into before I get
on the plane to go, the wind still
blowing & the rain coming & going,
and the water deep & dark with that
metallic hue, but it is unexpectedly
warm, as I am too despite the damp
& chill, I'm thinking of Paddy & the
moments spent alone, together, quiet,
or sharing some profound thought of his
he puts off on someone he has read—
& what he said when I asked if there
was anything I could send from "the
States" & he replied "What would I
need from there—" & I hesitatingly
suggest a book, and he lets me know,
as he already did a few days before,
that he's only studying "the one book
now, for my final exam—" with that
manly smile, unafraid of who he is
or who I might be or am—ah, it was
a grand visit, as they might say, &
now I want to run away before I stay
forever . . .